SONGBIRD CARVING
WITH ERNEST MUEHLMATT

SONGBIRD CARVING
WITH
ERNEST MUEHLMATT

World-class ribbon winner teaches you how to carve and paint ten favorite songbirds

by
Roger Schroeder
and
Ernest Muehlmatt

STACKPOLE BOOKS

Published by
STACKPOLE BOOKS
Cameron and Kelker Streets
P.O. Box 1831
Harrisburg, PA 17105

First paperback printing, December 1992

Printed in the U.S.A.

Library of Congress Cataloging-in-Publication Data

Muehlmatt, Ernest.
    Songbird carving with Ernest Muehlmatt.

    Bibliography: p.
    Includes index.
    1. Wood-carving – Patterns. 2. Decoration and
ornament – Animal forms. 3. Birds in art.
I. Schroeder, Roger, 1945–   II. Title.
TT199.7.M84   1987   731.4′62   86-14580
ISBN 0-8117-2573-1

To the Muehlmatts: Joan, Jeff, and Eric;
to the chickadee;
and to our friend, Judith Schnell.

Contents

Introduction

Ernest Muehlmatt is working on a trio of young chickadees. They sit on wispy, twisted branches, their glass eyes fixed in the timelessness imparted by the wooden sculpture. They are remarkable little birds, even though they do not defy gravity, nor do they raise their wings or even open their beaks in anticipation of food.

They are only wood, thin paint, and lines etched on their surfaces. Yet, despite the simplicity, they suggest more than process and materials. There is a look of something that, though not alive, has meaning—a feeling that suggests an event, perhaps a first night out or another presence in the chickadees' world. Exactly where that comes from is difficult to say. It might be the turn of a head, an eye that seems directed at the viewer, the soft texture of wood and paint, the puffiness of a feather grouping.

The process as Ernie describes it was simple. Several passes through a bandsaw blade and the birds became recognizable. A grinding tool and bits gave them their character by taking more wood away. A burning tool that sends heat through the handle to the tip put hundreds of minute grooves into the wood to suggest feathers. And after only twenty hours of work on the bodies, watery paints established the simple tones of the chickadees.

There was a parsimony of effort that carried over even to the composition itself. Pruning his work of excesses, Ernie has his chickadees on a single, forking piece of wood without leaves, without flowers at its base, without even a stone to ground the piece. What, then, brings out the essence of the birds and their habitat?

Answers, if there ever can be satisfactory ones when speaking of art that affirms and captures life in man-shaped forms, begin to be found not with the evidence of art or even its process, but instead with its geography.

It is better to ask, then, not what courses Ernie took in college, but instead what growing up in Southeastern Pennsylvania did to shape his thinking and later his birds. Though it is not so easy to understand what effect a father who was a plasterer and carpenter had on a little boy who liked to make lines on paper, it is easy to draw inferences from a father who became a florist and a son who would in later years describe

Ernie Muehlmatt burning in the details on a spruce grouse in his studio in Springfield, Pennsylvania.

The three immature chickadees Ernie is working on throughout the book.

A recently made chickadee adult, one of three thousand he has carved and painted in the last eighteen years.

birds as flowers that fly and arrange them in balanced compositions the Japanese call Ikebana.

Ernie did not move far from his birthplace in Alden, Pennsylvania. His property is in Springfield, which is made up of recent housing developments and large shopping centers. It is next to an undeveloped thousand acres of land, occupied by birds and deer and trees untouched for at least thirty years.

To avoid the shopping centers, he goes to Media. This Quaker-settled town of only six thousand residents, one half hour from what Philadelphians call Center City, still has trolley tracks, shiny with use, down its main street. Ernie likes its brick and stone buildings and its smallness. Interestingly, Ernie has carved so many birds in his eighteen years of shaping wood that each person in Media could possess one. He has carved so many chickadees alone that half the people there could own one.

Old Marple Road runs part of the two miles into Media. Ernie has lived on that road for forty-eight years. Greenhouses that his father worked in are still on the property. Even the building he worked in as a mechanic is there. It suggests a timber frame with board-and-batten siding, though the posts and beams are butted together rather than fitted with mortises and tenons. It is now Ernie's studio. The second floor of the building measures 30 by 40 feet. Two workbenches, each measuring 4 by 8 feet, take up nearly 5 percent of that space. Cabinets, countertops, a drafting table, a china cabinet, and a refrigerator use another 10 percent, and a dog without a pedigree often takes up 4½ square feet of floor.

A closer inventory begins to reveal what has been happening during Ernie's two decades of carving, half of that time in this building. Along with the power tools (some too heavy to move easily, others hand-held) of his trade, there are books of birds, most on shelves that sag with their weight, a few open on the tables to reveal photos, paintings, and monotone line drawings. There are mounted quail and a stuffed owl, all discolored by wood dust; glass eyes that stick out of plastic drawers; feet cast in lead; wood scraps that are recognizable as birds but which are called duds by Ernie; some smooth-bodied shorebirds dated in the early 1970s (one patriotically painted red, white, and blue); a brant decoy made of branches held together with string; hunting decoys made by a man with the unlikely name of Cigar Daisey; a Canada goose made by a carver with the Waspish name of E. Madison Mitchell. On one wall is a framed print of a meadow-lark, on another a faded piece of paper with a printed statement about Ernie that he is "King of the Bird Carvers" and adds, as fact, that he "runs the University of Bird Carving and Vinyl Upholstery School where he practices his finely honed ability of consumer rip-off."

There is a clutter of wood for bird bases, some from California, other pieces from the desert—some man-zanita and red cedar. There is an oak china closet with early work, and there are bronzes of birds and bird heads; a homemade burning tool housed in a large wooden box; two dozen tubes of paint, some leaking their colors, others almost unsqueezed; two lazy susan turntables and a hairdryer mounted upright. There are cans of brushes and trays of grinding bits. There are artifacts of old projects, one example being a cluster of bluejays started a few years after he occupied the building and still not finished. And there is the dust of projects in progress and the dust of projects done and sold.

There is what he calls a painting box—a platform for a mixing tray made out of cedar boards used in the greenhouse business. He nailed it together in 1968 and still uses it. He says it has a bit of color on it from all of the 6,000 birds he has carved.

On the rear wall is a perspective sculpture of the studio with the white dog on the floor, the tables clut-tered, the artifacts and mementoes in place.

This is Ernie's studio where he works at a parochial schedule that keeps him there for about ten hours each day, performing a quiet ballet between four areas where he roughs the bird into shape, grinds on it, burns its feathers under the halo of light cast by a flexible-arm lamp, paints its body, and dries it with that hairdryer.

Ernie himself, with his full head of gray-white hair

A diorama of Ernie's studio crafted by Jim McCullough in 1983. Ernie traded a meadowlark for it.

Ernie's painting box, made from greenhouse flats. He has used it for all of his eighteen years of carving and painting. He calls it his good luck painting box.

and a youthful face, might pass for a minister, a golf pro, even a flower designer (which he was). He is usually in cotton jeans and a pilling sweater with a small insignia that reads "Wild Wings Decoy Den," its sleeves pushed up his arms. He is laconic most of the time, working alone in the studio, interrupted only by the phone, an occasional visitor, a brother who still keeps the greenhouses in operation and comes up for hot water and coffee. But Ernie is ready to talk about his work that took shape from a background in flow-ers and advertising, as well as those creative leaps based on serendipities and chance encounters with other carvers, new tools, techniques, and wood.

There are pent-up feelings to share, the successes that came quietly, the passel of burdens with dead-lines and the insecurities of making enough money, the techniques that render a bird lifelike and those that don't.

This building was once the Pennsylvania Highway Shop No. 1. The studio is on the second floor. The first floor holds some tools but mostly wood for habitat and natural-looking bases.

He has enjoyed carving during the years when birds were given little detail and later were meticulously painted and burned, when decoys had flat bottoms and later took to flight and came back still later to the table. Ernie's changes have been less dramatic. But they are significant to understanding what puts life into a piece of wood while he spends about three thousand hours each year in the studio, repeating and refining the roughing, the grinding, the burning, the painting.

There are anecdotes he has to share, samplings of 58 years, glamorizing them only where they merit glamor, but refraining from cynicism when things went wrong.

There are glass sliding doors that lead in and out of the shop at the top of a wooden stairway on the outside of the building. Behind them he can be seen sitting at his painting area, putting the final washes of paint on the chickadees, the hairdryer blowing invisible warmth on them when he sets them down. He has prepared himself to talk while working on the birds. It will take most of the day to tell his story. As he explains his techniques during that time, he will isolate the small details of the style that identifies his work. He will discuss the discipline, the compulsion to produce, the need to try new poses.

There are connections he makes—how a cow's skull helped make five carved birds a prize-winning composition. There are admissions—he has carved birds he has never seen, even in photographs. There are inventions—gadgets he says look good but don't work well. And there are dreams—of owls in the night, fish during the day.

He's been ready for some time for someone to come through the sliding glass doors, take a seat next to him, and hear what it takes to be an artist with wood and paint.

Part One:
The Artist

Artist, Florist, Inventor

He squeezes two tubes of acrylic colors to make small blobs of thick paint that hang on the edge of his mixing tray. He adds water and stirs each separately. "It bothered me when that art school told me I'd be better off doing something else for a living." He says this evenly, easily, as if talking about someone else's career.

"I went to the Philadelphia College of Art. That's in Philadelphia," he adds, now mixing the colors in the white plastic tray that might have been left over from a beginner's paint set. A grayish color results. "It was an industrial and commercial arts school. At that time it had an excellent drawing program. There I learned how to draw." He breathes out a long pause. "Then I went to the Advertising and Art Students League. That was also in Philadelphia. What did I get out of it? I learned color. And I learned how to design a page of advertising. And whether you lay out a good ad page, or a flower arrangement," another pause, "or a well-designed bird, you've got to have a pleasing design."

He was in his early twenties then. But drawing was something he liked to do as a little boy. He remembers doing sketches when he was only four or five. It was work that was reinforced with praise. "I got pleasure out of drawing something and having people tell me it was good. It's like applause. A lady next door to where I lived as a kid worked for an advertising company, and she took me to work and showed me off." There at the office he was given his own desk where he could work.

Fifteen years later while in the army, he was stationed in the Aleutian Islands, which run like a interrupted chain off the end of Alaska into the Pacific Ocean. There G.I.s paid him to paint Varga-posed women over their beds. Varga was an illustrator who partially bared his sensual models; his work is being brought back on poster-sized prints.

He didn't have paints available on the base and had to borrow them or have them sent to him by his mother. For brushes he cut hair off a pet dog and attached it to a stick. He called them Windsor and Muehlmatts, a pun made at the expense of the manufacturer Windsor & Newton, a London-based firm that produces some of the finest sable-hair brushes available. Many of the brushes Ernie owns today come from that company, while his dog keeps all its hair.

He applies some of the grayish wash to one of the chickadees. There is little change in surface color. "After the service, I did some oil paintings. And after art school, I made a feeble attempt to get an art job. I could have had a job with a greeting card company that paid about 50 cents an hour or as a photo retoucher for a newspaper. But they were boring jobs, and my father needed me."

His father was a plasterer and a carpenter in Switzerland before he emigrated to the United States in 1910. He came, Ernie says, to help his uncle, who was a truck farmer near Media. Becoming ill during the flu epidemic of 1917 forced him to quit that and chauffeur for the wealthy residents of Philadelphia's Main Line. Finally he took a job as a truck mechanic for the Pennsylvania Department of Highways.

Pointing toward the glass doors with the end of his brush, he says, "This building I'm in was the first Pennsylvania Department of Highways shop. That bronze plaque over by the doors reads Shop No. 1. Where I'm working now was the office for the superintendent." Ernie begins to explain the events and connections that led to twenty years in the flower business. "The superintendent was an amateur gardener who liked to mess around with trees and rock gardens." Ernie shifts his weight so that he is facing the rear window of the studio. He indicates with the brush the hemlock trees that grow outside the building and are visible through the window. They were planted by the superintendent and Ernie's father. He says it was almost solid green with the three or four thousand hemlock trees they planted before a blight destroyed most of them.

"That's when they decided to build a greenhouse, the one right here on this property, in the year I was born, 1927. So the superintendent needed someone to work in the greenhouse, like a gentleman farmer, and that was my father." He poises the brush slightly above the chickadee he holds with a holding device consisting of a dowel and a clip. "We lived in Alden, about five miles from here. The superintendent left for a promotion, and we moved here and raised flowers, working in the retail business, doing flower arrangements for weddings and such. That was after I finished two years of art school, and my brother and I ran that business for about twenty years."

He finds it difficult to talk about being a florist, but he says, finally, "It was hard to get out of it. If I had dropped out earlier, while my father was still in it, the whole thing would have folded. It would have destroyed him, my mom, everything. And I couldn't hire someone to do what I was doing. I was doing the

Another view of Ernie's studio building. Framed with timbers in a post-and-beam fashion, it has board-and-batten siding.

Through the rear window of the studio can be seen a small valley with beech and hemlock trees. Ernie sometimes sees deer there.

flower arranging; I knew growing, watering, feeding—who could replace me?"

He speculates that if circumstances had been different, he would have gone to medical school. "I would have been a half-decent plastic surgeon with my art background." He lets out an ironic laugh.

He next ponders what he could not have done. He describes writing as agony, even writing a letter. But, he says he works on "visual stuff. If I read something, it's not there. But I can look at a picture of a bird and remember which of the fifty books I have lined up it's in. Even audio things I hear go in one ear and out the other. But I guess you have to be an artist to remember what you see. I can remember a bird sitting outside my window and the position he's in. It sticks. Then I can work up a good pattern from what I saw. I can close my eyes and still see it."

He remembers birds he saw forty years ago during his stay on the Aleutian Islands. He woke up one morning and saw a snowy owl on his Quonset hut. He thinks he remembers other birds, puffins among them. "I think that was when I got interested in birds," he suggests. Forty years later another kind of owl returned, a victim of an automobile, to become his most challenging project.

Wildlife is not uncommon on his property. A great variety of wildfowl and deer make their homes in the woods that surround two sides of his land. The Catholic Church of Philadelphia is responsible for this largest undeveloped parcel of land within fifteen miles west of Philadelphia. In Ernie's words, it has "rolling hills, outcroppings of rocks, hemlocks and tulip poplars, and marshy areas. It's very similar to the Poconos.

"There's a place in those woods called Crow Rock that I used to play on when I was a kid. It's got a cave. We always thought Indians used it as a burial ground. There's even a rock that sticks a hundred feet into the air."

Down Old Marple Road, there are the stony remains of the sandstone quarry that supplied the stone for many of the older houses in the area. Beyond that is Media. That town is where most of Ernie's friends are. He calls it his "favorite town in all the world. I feel comfortable in Media. I shop there rather than in a mall. There's a small, hometown feeling. I wouldn't feel happy in a big city. I go into Philadelphia very seldom. And when I do, I can't wait to get out of there.

"But over the last fifty-eight years, about forty-eight of them on this property, there's been a vast change.

Ernie's house. In the foreground is a 1945 Army jeep he uses to travel into the nearby town of Media. Surrounding the house are Norway spruce, tulip poplars, and white pines.

This is an early wren Ernie made. Nearly all the details were achieved with paints, even the eyes.

There was one big farm after another. It would have reminded you of the Lancaster area in Pennsylvania. Go back seventy years ago; there were still a lot of dirt roads. That's when my father was doing his truck farming. He would take a wagon of produce into Philadelphia.

"I went to school five miles from here. There was nothing but farmland, pastures, and cornfields. It was a lot of fun growing up in the farming atmosphere. I remember seeing what I today know as red-tailed hawks, turkey buzzards, owls. I remember when we had about forty pheasants roosting in the pine trees near the house. That was back in 1950 when we had it built. Now we see deer and no pheasants. We have woodcocks, but no bobwhite quail or grouse. And we still have all those tulip poplars in the woods."

It was from that tree, a straight-growing species with a yellowish white wood that is easily worked with tools and used for the unseen parts of furniture, that Ernie carved his first bird. He thinks it was a

A spotted sandpiper, one of the very first birds he made. This one was carved around 1968. It copies birds made by Robert Hogg. Hogg was a Philadelphia cabinetmaker whose carvings helped inspire Ernie.

wren. "I didn't know what wood to use or what tools I needed. But I got a piece from the woods. It was tulip poplar. The wood was a branch with an additional branch coming out. That was the tail and the rest was the bird. It was a complete disaster."

Prior to that, his wife had given him a sandpiper made by a Philadelphia cabinetmaker. A short time after that, he went south to a birdcarving exhibition held in Salisbury, Maryland. It later became the World Championship Wildfowl Carving Competition. That was in 1968. The same year he and his brother decided to quit the retail commitment and bought an answering machine to share the fact. But his brother continues a wholesale business of seasonal flowers in the three greenhouses on the property: impatiens, primrose, and ranunculus for the spring and summer,

A pair of mourning doves Ernie made in 1970. Photo courtesy of the Ward Foundation.

An early cardinal carved in 1967 or 1968.

poinsettias for the winter. Ernie decided to apply as much of his time as he could to carving birds.

He calls that Salisbury show interesting and fun. "I saw things that turned me on, and everyone seemed real busy and had lots of orders and couldn't handle any more work. Everything was sold out. It seemed to be in demand and it was something I could do."

He recalls carving birds in the boiler room for the greenhouses. The day started at four in the morning. In the boiler room, he had a small shop set up with mostly hand tools but also a bandsaw he had found in someone's trash. He didn't have enough money to buy one, even a used one, and he used a saber saw for a time to cut out the profiles of birds from wood. He compares this to applying a chainsaw to a small carving.

He says he still had to do some greenhouse work and run the produce stand that presently exists at the foot of the steep, S-curving driveway. He would work until 9 A.M., work in the greenhouse, break for dinner, and from 5:30 P.M. to 9 P.M. continue his carving. He did that for a few years, but the boiler room was too cramped, so he ended up in the garden center, taking over half the building while the rest was used to sell vegetables. There he spent ten years, years he calls lonely, and even offered carving classes in the building. "I'd have ten people, $10 a head, and make $100 a night. But that's part of paying your dues, isn't it? I work a long day now, but it's not as hard as it used to be."

He talks about his present setup in the converted highway building that still has a garage below next

This pheasant was carved around the same time as the cardinal. Ernie describes the painting as stylized.

A pair of nuthatches on a piece of chestnut wood Ernie got from behind the studio building.

to the room where he keeps wood for the bases or branches on which he mounts his birds. What he describes is a choreography that has him making smooth transitions from one area to another as the bird begins as a block of wood and ends, like his chickadees, soft- and expectant-looking. What he calls dirty work is done at a bandsaw and a stationary motor that rotates a sanding attachment. "That's in one little corner where I have vacuums to suck up the dust. Then I go to my Foredom station." There he mounted from the ceiling three motors with flexible shafts that lead to handpieces. The Foredom is a tool used by most carvers today who, instead of using knives, prefer a high-speed rotary bit in the handpiece to sculpt the wood quickly. There Ernie has a music stand that holds nearly vertical pictures of birds he refers to when shaping the wood with the Foredom, which he

has started to replace with a higher-speed grinder. The Foredom rotates detachable bits at 14,000 rpm. It was developed by jewelers and dental technicians for shaping metal and teeth. But the dental industry has come out with higher-rpm grinders. Today one product can rotate a grinding stone at 45,000 rpm.

"I have one main light at the Foredom station that casts a shadow on the bird to get a better idea of the bumps and contours on the bird." He says he has the same kind of light at the next stage, the burning area. There, with sophisticated rheostat-controlled burning pens, he draws with heat the feather barbs and patterns on the contoured body of the bird he's working on. "You need an almost oblique light to cast a shadow," he says. "Any other light would blot out what you're doing. You need a shadow to see some of the light burns I put on the bird."

But at the next area, he wants no shadows. This is his painting station, which has its own table and turntables on that for paints and the birds themselves. There he has a fluorescent light above and lights with aluminum reflectors to the left and right of him. Like most other bird artists, he paints the bird as if it were seen in open daylight. Exhibition and competition halls will create their own shadows on the bird, so it's best to paint the wood without the interference of light and dark patches on it.

Those are the four main areas between which he quietly moves. A much less used area has a drafting table against a wall and adjacent to a refrigerator that always has milk for coffee and beer for the afternoons and evenings. He says the drafting table is there for drawing and painting, though he does little with

Ernie is at his Foredom station working on the wing of a great horned owl he made in 1985.

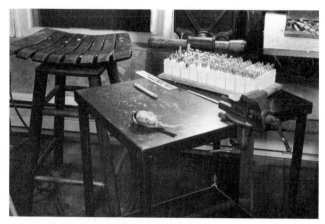

Another photo of the Foredom station, with a chickadee study skin and a large assortment of grinding bits.

flatwork art and seldom drafts a composition of bird and habitat.

"It takes a lot of different skills, don't you think, to become a good bird carver" he says, brushing the gray-ish wash on the breast of one of the chickadees. "Well, let's see. You have to be an ornithologist, I suppose. You have to be fairly good with colors and paints. You have to be a carpenter and know how to handle wood." Ernie, like other carvers, has tried a range of woods from hard to soft varieties, some from the Far East, others from swamps. Each responds differently to grinders, burning pens, and paints. "You have to be a good designer. And I would think you have to have a little bit of botany in your background." He refers to artificially made leaves, branches, and flowers that may complement a bird on a base. "You have to be able to work with plaster and body putties when you make habitat like rocks and earth. If you make your own bases, you have to be a cabinetmaker. What else?"

He starts to say that's it, when he remembers, "Oh, yes, a photographer if you want to take nature shots and metalworker if you make metal leaves or grasses or if you have a bird supported by a feather tip like a bird flying through grasses or a hummingbird with a metal beak in a flower." Ernie has made neither of these, though others have.

"It requires a lot of different skills and discipline, a lot of discipline. You're not going to get anything done if you don't sit your fanny down and force yourself to do it. You have to treat this like a job. It's so easy when you're working by yourself to go out to lunch or do some wildfowl studying. You just have to sit and crank it out every day, even Sundays. Most guys in this work Sundays." He remembers a statement made in art school. "The only artist who would starve is the lazy artist," he says, dipping the brush for a long moment in the paint wash.

Being a bird carver, however, is isolating work, and that has its problems, he admits. As he explains it, "You sit around here for months on end, and you don't talk to too many people. And you can't ask your son" (he has two) "or your wife to evaluate your work." Ernie's solution is to go to competitions and exhibitions to hear criticism. The competitions in particular excite him. "It makes me feel good that my works are accepted. It's like getting applause, especially if you win something." He recently created a piece that had not been put into a competition. It was a mother blue-jay protectively spreading its wings over three babies.

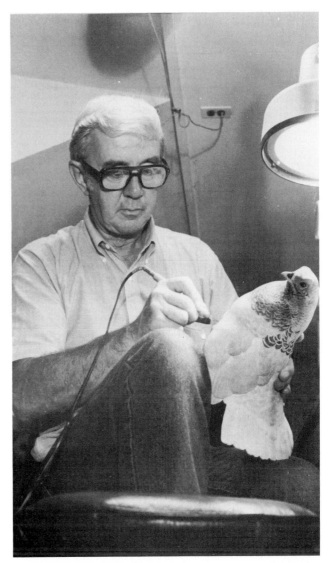

Ernie is at his burning station working on a spruce grouse. He says this bird was one of his favorite projects. The feather patterns on the bird were done with heat instead of paint.

The painting station, a yard-sale hairdryer, and brushes, which Ernie says he loves to buy.

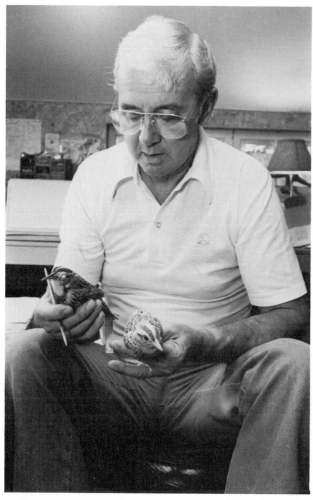

At the painting station working on an immature meadowlark for the Danbury Mint. Photo courtesy of Wildfowl Carving and Collecting

All four birds were carved from one piece of wood. Of that, he says, "I wasn't too pleased with them. But I took them to this show in Salisbury [Maryland] and right away people were telling me how nice they were." He sold the piece almost immediately and was commissioned to do another one.

He has ambivalent feelings toward the traveling, though. "As a bird carver, you have the opportunity to travel, but then you get to a point where it's not fun to travel anymore. It's almost like a job." During one year he will travel twice to Maryland, once to Kansas City, Kansas, twice to Florida, once to Charleston, South Carolina, and one time to San Diego, California. "It's a job to pack your stuff and have everything arrive in one piece, do your show, pack up again. I guess it's fun and work at the same time. But I always get something out of a show, even if it's a financial disaster. A new contract, a new idea to try."

Ernie has a long history of "new ideas." His have come mostly in the form of inventions. "How did I get into inventions," he says without ending with a question mark. "I guess to make some extra money when I got married. I wrote a couple of articles for *Popular Science*. I did two inflatable greenhouses and a geodesic dome." But history gives credit for it to Buckminster Fuller. "I did a ski tow made out of odds and ends and run off the back end of an automobile." He seems ready to laugh, but doesn't. "It didn't work, but it was interesting reading." Now he laughs. "Oh, the domes worked all right if you had the right weather conditions. It wasn't the greatest thing in a blizzard or a snow storm, but it *looked* good. I had my inflatable greenhouse up for more than a year."

He describes it as a bubble of air with no superstructure. Yet, there was little air pressure involved. He says the difference in air pressure between being on top of a ten-story building and ground level was enough to hold the building up. "We could hold it up with a little blower. But you had to worry about getting in and out of it. There are still a lot of them around. I was one of the first guys to build one of them. I guess I was thinking of a cheaper way to make a greenhouse and grow things. The blower was a squirrel cage blower. I used one I got off a home heater. And the structure had an airlock door so you would go in, close it and go through another. *Popular Science* magazine came out in the fall when my flowers where in bloom and took a picture. Then they had an artist paint it, and it was the cover for the magazine." The January, 1961, cover had no flowers but instead a playground slide; a picnic table; a young woman in tight, severely cutdown jeans; and a man in the airlock removing a winter coat. Outside, snow whites the painting and a frosty snowman with a top hat roundly squats in the right-hand corner. Black letters read that the air bubble can be build for $50. A black and white photo inside the magazine shows a very thin Ernie holding a pot of flowers.

He has been reading a magazine article profiling wildlife artist Robert Bateman. Canadian-born and three years younger than Ernie, Bateman lives in Milton, Ontario. The magazine lies open on the painting table. He puts his brush down across the mixing tray, reaches for it, and reads paragraphs aloud. He summarizes, repeating his feelings about discipline. "Most guys to be successful have to be disciplined, like this painter Bateman here in this article. He's a seven-day-a-week worker, the same as I am. He's always up at 8:15 and in his studio by 9. I beat him by a half an hour there. And he will paint until noon, then go for a run in the woods and a light nap and back to work. I don't do that. I eat, then come right out to work again. Then he goes after supper and works until 11. That's the same as I do. Every guy who's half-way successful at this does the same thing."

His eyes follow a finger as it searches one of the pages. "Here's another thing I agree with. Bateman says that in order to be an artist, you have to make at least ten thousand mistakes." Ernie looks up from the page. "So to be successful, you'd better get ready to make mistakes. I'm not afraid to make them. He does the same thing I do. He plunges right into something. I've made easily ten thousand mistakes.

"It would be interesting to take a survey of artists and how they think alike. I think Bateman couldn't wait to get out of school." He reflects for a moment. "It would be nice to be rewarded when you do something right. In school, you're doing things wrong all the time. At that one art school, there was a lot of practical stuff, which I had trouble with. I guess that's why they thought I should try something else."

Ernie wonders if he has a learning disability. "I couldn't do math worth a damn. But I wasn't a bad student in high school. We had calculus and that was like telling me to fly to the moon. English was terrible, but art was great. My son Jeff is a good artist. He

A model of Ernie's inflatable plastic greenhouse featured in Popular Science *magazine. It was exhibited at the Philadelphia Flower Show in a desert setting.*

draws, paints decoys. He likes mechanical things. My other son, Eric, is a dean's list guy all the time. He doesn't work too hard at college. It's easy for him."

He goes back to perusing the page, finding other similarities in work habits and techniques. He jabs at the page with his finger. "Here's another thing. He paints the way I do. He calls it a limited palette of basically four colors."

Muted Palette

Ernie nods his head approvingly. "Bateman does the same thing with his palette," he says, "but he calls it a limited palette. That means the same as what I call it, a muted palette. It's essentially white, burnt umber, ultramarine blue, and yellow ochre for 90 percent of a painting. And if he has to use any other color, it's cadmium red, which I would use for a cardinal; cadmium yellow, which I would use for a meadowlark's chest; phthalo blue, which I don't know anything about." He disguises a quiet laugh. "And phthalo rose."

He pushes the magazine aside. "I guess I could whip up those odd colors with my burnt siennas and mute them down a little bit. But it says he uses so little of them, they usually dry up in the tubes before they're used up. I have a lot of those crazy colors," he says, pointing at an unorganized cluster of tubes.

"What colors do I use?" he asks himself. "They're ultramarine blue, burnt umber, yellow ochre, and burnt sienna. I'll bet you can do almost every bird there is," he says, getting out of his chair. He returns with the books contained in the *Audubon Society Master Guide to Birding*, three volumes of color photos and paintings of North American birds. Seated, he opens

one book and lets the page edges slip along a thumb. "Let me see something in this bird book. In the songbird category," he announces loudly, "a robin would be handled very nicely with these four colors. For the red I would use cadmium red. Then there's a red start, a rose breasted grosbeak, a female cardinal."

His thumb continues its search. "Now we're getting into the orange birds, which you couldn't do very well without other colors. A meadowlark would be handled nicely. All your sparrows. Here are the birds that would be right up my alley: nuthatch, brown creeper, downy woodpecker, except for the red on that dude. Almost all the game birds: quail, woodcocks, California quail, perfect." He is excited. "Swallows, a purple martin—an absolutely gorgeous bird. All your pigeons. Hawks? A kestrel would be great, just super. It has burnt siennas, yellow ochres." He's found the seabirds. "All your seabirds and shorebirds, every one of them different shades of grays, bluish grays, brownish grays—every one of them that ever flew.

"Look at that great horned owl," he says, pressing down the pages of a book. He remembers the one that he carved, the one that made him breathe in too much wood dust, the one that kept him awake at night, the one he feared he would not finish. But the fears are gone, and he says, "You could use four of my colors for that." He did. "Burnt umber, burnt sienna, ultramarine blue, and yellow ochre."

More pages are fanned away under his thumb. He points out a picture of a bobwhite quail. He's done many. Five of them became a World Championship piece. "For the backs of the ones I carve, I use burnt umber and ultramarine blue. On the head," he has no trouble remembering, "I use a mixture of burnt umber, ultramarine blue in equal parts to make a deep, deep brown. And when I put that on the browns I burned on the back," he says, referring to his burning in feather patterns dark enough to match their actual brown and black colors, "it gives me an almost velvety black. On a woodcock I do, I can use the burnt umber right out of the tube. If it's too bright, I can tone it down with a little ultramarine blue."

He's found a picture of an avocet and jabs a finger at it. "Burnt sienna up here," he says, indicating the neck and head, "a little yellow there. The back is a mixture of burnt umber and ultramarine blue." He smiles widely.

But he admits that there are other colors he needs. White is done with gesso and water. A liquid paint containing white pigment, gesso has been used as a primer for wood, canvas, plaster, and other porous surfaces. Fast-drying, resistant to oil and water, and pore-filling, it is applied by many carvers who use it as a base for acrylics, the paints that Ernie uses.

Stable, durable, adhesive are adjectives that can be applied to acrylic paints, a relatively new medium for artists. Had a da Vinci or a Rembrandt used these plastic resins, their paintings would never have become brittle or developed hairline cracks across them, nor would a portrait have darkened. Emulsified in water, the resin consists of fine particles held in suspension. When the water evaporates, these particles flow together to form a clear, flexible film.

Exterior painters of the 1920s mural movement did their share to hasten the need for more durable paints. Linseed oil, the vehicle for the oil paints that were used up to that time, is unstable and becomes porous. A chemical breakdown occurs within the paint, and a process takes place not unlike the one on the surface of the aging human body. The plastic acrylic paints resist this and provide a cohesiveness to the surfaces to which they are applied.

He piles the Audubon books together and breathes

An early smooth chickadee done with a thick mixture of matte medium and paint. A wide brush would push and pile the paint up to give a bumpy look. A wet brush would later pull wet paint from under the chin down toward the breast. Also, the eyes were painted in.

The back of the chickadee. A flared brush would drag a mix of black and matte medium over the wings to give the look of feather barbs.

deeply. He says he began with acrylics because he had a set given to him by a cousin. "I thought they were good because they dried right away, and since I worked real fast, that was the main reason I continued with them. What I read indicated they were color-fast and long-lasting and held up very well.

"I started using a wash technique. That's putting thinned-down layers of paint on the bird. Acrylics lend themselves very well to that. You can make layer after layer."

He says when he started carving he used matte medium, a vehicle for dry pigments that leaves a glossy surface. It is often mixed in with acrylics out of the tube. This helped him blend colors. As he describes the process, "I did what I called 'pulling.' That's where you might put a black and a white down on the bird and then take a wide brush and poke it into the black and pull feathers from one area into another.

A later chickadee with glass eyes and some carving. Ernie says that many of his birds made in the late 1970s had a porcelain look to them.

A recent chickadee and a holding device to facilitate painting. Made of tupelo, the chickadee's dark areas were burned with a burning tool, and the light areas were painted with light washes of watered-down acrylics.

Take this little chickadee here." He lifts it up by its stick-and-clip holding device and points to the bird's black-capped head. "You would put your white in here on the cheek, then take a black brush with black paint, and while the white is still wet, poke it into the white and drag it back. The white paint would follow you back in little tiny strings and hairs and give you the effect of white feathers overlapping the black area."

He returns the chickadee to the turntable. "I think most bird carvers use acrylics." Most do use this plastic resin because of its fast drying time, several minutes, and the ease with which mistakes can be corrected. Oil paints require turpentine as a vehicle, which sometimes brings out allergic reactions, and the drying time can be days instead of minutes. But those carvers who do use oil paints praise their blending properties and the soft appearance imparted to a bird.

Ernie says he did portraits with oil paints. "I didn't enjoy them. It all depends on what you get used to. The guys who use oils claim they can blend them better, and they probably can. But they stay wet forever. With those slow-drying oils, I had a tendency to get my work muddy looking. But with acrylics, you can wash up with water; the paints are really permanent; they don't fade like oils; and they don't yellow. They're a good paint to use."

He recalls modular colors and finds several tubes. They were available until four or five years ago. "Few people used them. For example, you had eight different shades of yellow. It was a great system, but it didn't go over with painters, and it was abandoned. But they would have every color broken down into eight values." He picks up a tube. "They did the same with the greens, the reds, the blues. It was a little hard to get used to, but I used that system for years and years."

He explains that base yellow in the old system was what is now called burnt umber. Higher up the scale to a number 5 is now called bronze yellow. A number 8 would be cadmium yellow. A base blue would today be called blue black. A number 8 blue would be a cobalt blue.

"So," he says, elongating the single syllable, "now that modular paints are no longer with us, I use this muted palette thing with burnt umber, burnt sienna, yellow ochre, and ultramarine blue, and I can handle almost all my work with these colors using transparent washes. But I don't mix gesso with any of my colors." Nor does he prime the wood with gesso, which would load up his burning lines and hide the shades of color affected by them. He will, however, apply thin coats of gesso to lightly burned areas before putting down a wash of color. He explains that instead of lightening a blue with gesso by mixing the two together, he will first put the white gesso on the bird and then apply a light blue wash, using the ultramarine blue of his muted palette.

"The white on the bird gets the light blue," Ernie says. "If it's too brilliant a blue, I'll go to the opposite color on the color wheel, which is, let me see, burnt sienna or burnt umber, mix a light wash and go over the blue." The color wheel is used by all painters of canvas to determine how the mixing of basic colors results in other colors. What are called the primary colors are red, yellow, and blue. Mixing red and yellow results in orange; yellow and blue make green; and blue and red make purple.

"So that's like mixing blue and brown together." Ernie continues, "except I'm mixing them on the bird instead of on my palette. If you're doing a bluebird, you could use just burnt sienna and ultramarine blue in certain areas, but first you have to undercoat the entire bird with thinned-down gesso; blue doesn't show up unless it has that underneath. But not blue and white together," he repeats himself. "That would leave a chalky, dead-looking bird."

He talks more about bluebirds. "In some areas, you could use blue straight out of the tube. For the grayish blues, it's alternate washes of burnt sienna and ultramarine blue with less ultramarine blue to mute down the blue. You just have to watch it as you go along."

He compares his washes to pieces of colored cellophane laid on top of each other. Other carvers have compared them to highlighter markings. "All the colors I use are transparent with no white in them." He reaches for a tube of cobalt blue. It has hardly been squeezed. "This color has white in it," he says, reading the label. "It has blue pigment, and titanium oxide is the white. Any of these colors with white in them gives you an opaque color. But I like to look through my layers of paint right down to the wood."

He has simplified his mixing of wash coats for bluebirds. "If they're too blue, you add some burnt sienna. That's the brown wash. If they're getting too brown, kill them with a wash of ultramarine blue. Back to my chickadees here; I've mixed up two washes, one of burnt umber and one of ultramarine blue, then put on alternate layers until I get the tone I want. But they're

Ernie compares putting acrylic washes over one another to laying down thin sheets of cellophane on top of each other.

A quiet hairdryer dries the washes put on the birds.

going to look darker than they really are while they're wet, so they have to be bone dry. Otherwise you can't tell."

He has speeded up that drying process with a hairdryer. He bought the one he uses at a yard sale for about $2. He shuts it off and picks it up, revolving it in his hands. He's found what he was looking for. It's great. It's slow and makes a gentle hot breeze and can be run all day. Putting it back and turning it on again, he complains that quiet dryers are almost impossible to purchase. He points out that his runs at 200 watts compared to the 1,200 watts of most contemporary ones. "You can listen to your music and it doesn't interfere with your concentration."

He frowns suddenly. "I must be getting senile. I have some bluebirds right here." Three immature birds are in his shop packed in an unsealed cardboard box. They sit expectantly on a branching piece of wood, two with their mouths open. He places the trio on his painting table. They lack the bright blues and rusty

Three immature bluebirds with the breasts mottled with white and a bluish gray of ultramarine blue and burnt umber.

The backs of the bluebirds. The spots were not painted on but left as unpainted areas on the birds. This technique give a softer effect than if the spots had been painted on over the blue gray.

oranges of the adult birds. Instead, bluish browns color their backs, and their breasts are mottled with whites and grays. "I can show you the colors right here," he says, adjusting his glasses. "All the grays were accomplished from the combination of ultramarine blue and burnt sienna. See this bright color on the wings? That's almost straight ultramarine blue." He talks about the breast area being what he calls a reddish or warm gray. "That's more burnt sienna than ultramarine blue."

He explains his use of gesso on the baby bluebirds. "An entire bird was given one thin coat of gesso. Each white spot on the breast and back had eight different applications of gesso. They stood out as super white before I applied washes of other colors. A little yellow ochre would get rid of a chalky whiteness. For these areas of real light blue on the wings I wanted a strong white underneath, so I had at least four coats of white to get it really white so it would shine through the blue I put on top. Remember, I don't mix white with blue. I put it underneath. And each coat is so light that wherever you stop, you don't get a hard line of color. That's another advantage of using thin acrylic washes. They're so light you don't really notice where each coat stops."

Still, he tests the intensity of his washes on pieces of white paper. "Most of my washes are real, real light. The average wash is so light, you don't even see it, but the next coat you'll see it, and the third and fourth time the color really jumps out at you."

He finds that correcting his colors is easy with this strategy. "Leave it a few days," he advises of a project, "and come back and see something that needs to be touched up. Just wash it with different colors. It's a

neat way to work. But you have to think ahead all the time; think of the feather groups. I guess you have to carve and draw and recarve and redraw to see if it all fits together. I guess you draw the feathers in ten, fifteen times before you have it carved. There's nothing worse than carving a group of feathers and finding out you don't have enough room to draw in the individual ones."

He describes what he calls his painting strategy for a baby bluebird or chickadee. "I start out in my normal sequence. The rump is light, the secondary feathers a little bit darker, the primary feathers a little bit darker yet, the tail a shade darker still. The back is the last thing I'll do. That's a shade darker yet. Then I'll go over the whole thing with my original mix as a wash. Then I'll shade each of the primary and secondary feathers to give them contrast, then outline the secondaries with white." On the bill he applies yellow ochre.

He pauses with a quizzical look. "Did I tell you about warm and cool colors?" He shakes his head. "Burnt sienna and ultramarine blue, my favorite colors, will give you a warm gray." He hesitates, rethinking what he may have mixed several thousand times. "Raw umber and blue would give you a cool gray." He has touched on an area long known to European and Oriental painters who exploited warm and cool colors to suggest spatial depth. Simple experiments of contrasting one color to another will bear this out. A green hue will seem cool if surrounded by yellow, but warm when surrounded by blue-green. Hues containing a high proportion of blue, in the range of violet to green, appear cooler than those with a high content of yellow or red, which is in the green-yellow to red-violet range.

Feather edges are achieved by spreading a brush out and dabbing lines of white on the bird.

Painting the primaries on an immature meadowlark with a mix of ultramarine blue and burnt umber, two of the colors that make up Ernie's muted palette. Photo courtesy of Wildfowl Carving and Collecting.

The white chalkiness of the gesso can be toned down by applying a light wash of something like burnt umber.

Ernie explains his understanding of cool and warm colors. "The guys who do flatwork art, if they use cool colors in the shadows of their paintings, get your eyes to focus differently on them. Did you ever notice when you see red lettering on a piece of green paper how the red seems to pop right out at you? The red seems to stand up an eighth of an inch." He has learned of the different nerve endings in the retina. These cause the eye to focus differently on red than on green. "You focus red at a different part of the retina than you do for the greens and cool colors. That's what gives you the depth of red on green.

"So artists who want to add extra depth will paint certain parts of the painting with cool colors, maybe a greeny gray to make something recede. If a wildlife artist were doing a bobwhite quail and wanted it to pop out from the canvas, he would paint the quail with warm colors like burnt sienna or a warm gray.

When doing feathers, as on this baby meadowlark, Ernie leaves a white edge made by the gesso applied before the other washes. Photo courtesy of Wildfowl Carving and Collecting.

The breast of this chickadee was done with gesso and washed with raw umber to tone down the whiteness. The head, after it was burned, was washed with warm black. Then white feathers were flicked on the head.

Note the white edges left on this chickadee. These are made up of the original white.

Ernie's painting strategy has the rump lightly burned, the secondary feathers burned slightly darker, the primary feathers burned darker yet, and the tail darker than that. The back is the last area to be painted.

With a green background of, say, leaves or grasses, the quail would seem to pop out."

He smiles broadly. "Does this make any sense? What about a carving? You could do the same thing on one of these little birds." He lifts up the bluebird trio. "If you had an area you had meant to put more contours in and you had forgotten to do it, you could add shading or shadows." He points to the flank of one of the immature birds. "Suppose you wanted to put a little dip in there. You could shade it with cool colors and add warm colors on the high areas around it. You could get a three-dimensional effect that wasn't there. It would look carved."

He returns the bluebirds on their branch to the box, gently letting the base slip to the bottom. He returns to painting the chickadees. He says that after he has finished a bluebird or chickadee with the basic washes and has painted its beak, he will finish the bird with a process he calls feather flicking. "I'll do this on the heads and rumps. It softens the look," he says, putting more of the gray wash on the breast of a chickadee.

But he digresses when he says, "I used to use real sable brushes when I painted feathers on smooth birds. Windsor & Newton, series 7," he adds. "I used a lot of series 7 brushes. I needed them for feather barbs and edges. But now all that detailing is done with the burning pen, so there's no need for a fine-pointed brush. Now I buy Robert Simmond synthetic brushes. I use a lot of number 4s and 5s, or Windsor & Newton synthetic brushes."

He prefers Robert Simmond brushes, a series 785, buying them by the dozen at a local art store. He says they are short-lived with use and being in water all day. When he starts to paint a new series of birds, such as the chickadees, he'll start with a new brush. He says he can't resist buying brushes, though some of the Windsor & Newton brushes, made in England, cost $25 apiece, or more if made of red sable. But he concedes that a $1 brush will serve the same purpose.

He reaches over and lifts a brush out of the coffee can of brushes near his paint turntable. He presses it on a piece of white notepaper he has used to test the intensity of his washes, now covered with wide swatches of thin browns and blues. "This brush was trimmed with a razor blade for flicking feathers, say on the top of one of these chickadees' heads. It makes the head look softer. And I'll do it on the rump of a bird."

He holds the trimmed bristles upright. "I'll load it up with paint and spread it out, and it stays flared out.

The method Ernie used for painting his one-time smooth birds before burning. The brush was loaded with paint and dragged across the bird. Ernie says this took a fair amount of skill.

Then I use the edge of it," he says, as he presses the brush on a paper towel, "and it stays flared out. See how it stays nice and chisel-shaped? It remains that way on the bird. So you just flick some rows across the top of the head or the rump with some watered-down gesso and go over that with the original wash."

He recalls how a brush like this one was used to paint the appearance of feathers on an unburned bird. "Each little hair on the end of the flared-out brush would leave a fine little line. So with each stroke you'd make fifty barb lines. This was in the old days before burning," he says, as if a great many years had passed since he changed to scorching the wood in place of painting it.

He replaces the brush in the can. "I'd do a bird in half the time with paints. That's why I used to say that burning was for guys who couldn't paint."

Burning for Color

"Stay," he commands the slightly swaying chickadee, as he puts its wire-clip-dowel support in front of the hairdryer.

"I'm known for burning now, but I resisted it. In those days I'd paint all the feather barbs in. I was probably the last guy to come around to burning," he shares. "I was still doing smooth birds while everybody else was burning. So I said one day, 'What the hell, I'll give it a try.' That was shortly before, let me see. . . ." The pause is brief. "I started burning for color after I saw Tan's work. That was at Easton. I was still painting in the conventional way. It was too tempting to resist anymore."

Easton is a small town on Maryland's Chesapeake side with a population of less than seven thousand. In November of each year the community brings in twenty-five thousand visitors to the biggest waterfowl festival in North America. It is the ultimate in bird consciousness. Store manikins take on duck heads, shops sell bird art, schools and civic centers house carvers and painters exhibiting and demonstrating, and plates of oysters are sold on the streets. Even the expected cold November rains do not deter visitors who stand in line for up to two hours waiting to see the artists and their works for sale.

Tan Brunet also goes to Easton to sell birds. Cajun-born, resident of Galliano, Louisiana, living on Bayou LaFourche, Tan is recognized as one of the best of the contemporary duck carvers. He won't hesitate to tell you that, appending his signature with "Five times World Champion." Five times he won the title for floating pairs of decorative ducks at the Ocean City, Maryland, Wildfowl Carving Championships.

Tan is more than a winner of ribbons. With an entourage of friends from the parishes along the bayou, he cuts quickly through the seriousness of competitions, neutralizing the ceremonial atmosphere with jokes and occasional leaps into flotation tanks where ducks judged for their decoy attitude start bobbing like apples gone mad.

But the carver in Brunet is intensely serious. In a shop crowded with large, stuffed chairs and a single table arrayed with nearly everything needed to carve, from rasps to mounted birds, Brunet and his son Jett have produced some of the finest handmade waterfowl ever to float in their quietly composed way.

Finely rendered, they are meticulously burned and precisely painted with oil colors.

Ernie looks out the window into the hemlocks on the sloping ground between his studio and Old Marple Road. "When I was down at Easton, I forget what year it was, about five or six years ago, I was located right next to Tan. He had a pintail hen. He came up in a hurry from Louisiana and he hadn't finished it." Continuing with a wash coat of ultramarine blue on a chickadee that looks slightly more brown than gray, Ernie says, "Tan burns very precisely and does a little bit of shading with the burning pen. And the pintail wasn't painted, and all weekend long I listened to people say how nice and soft it looked, and he would explain he didn't have a chance to paint it, and people would say it looked pretty that way, that it would be a shame to put paint on it. Which it would have been.

"It would have been a shame to wipe out all that nice shading," Ernie says as if for the first time. "I thought it would be nice to burn a bird by regulating the heat on the burning pen and then try to burn as carefully as I could to get different tones of brown." He inhales deeply and continues. "So I came home and did an owl. It was the first bird I did that way, and it was sold to David Rockefeller at an Audubon show."

Ernie says that this one was painted. "It was 90 percent burned with very little paint. Over the years of burning I still do just as much burning and shading, but with more and more paint. So the first ones had very little paint. Now it's probably up to 50 percent paint. It's a good technique," he says, as if he were speaking of someone else's procedure. "It works exceptionally well for the game birds like grouse, woodcocks, even great horned owls.

"Here, you can see it on this bird over here." Off his stool and over to the table covered with burning tips and books and blocks of wood (some of which look like birds—birds with legs and birds without), a camera, and reading glasses too close to the edge of the tabletop, he returns with a meadowlark mounted on a postlike block of cedar. It has a strangely illustrated look with half its face and one flank scored with black and brown lines and dark markings. The other half of the face and one flank are furrowed with thin channels left by a grinding stone, leaving a neck with what appears to be stretch marks. One shoulder also has the dark markings that are characteristic of this yellow and black species of songbird.

He puts the bird and its base down gently in front of him. After a short, reflective pause, he says, "I just had

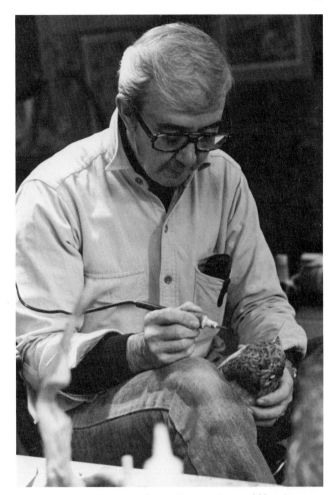

A photo of Ernie taken around 1980. He was using an old burning pen to burn the colors on a screech owl, one of his first projects that replaced paint with burn lines. The owl is now owned by David Rockefeller.

Ernie calls the Carolina wren done in the early 1980s a fairly easy project for testing one's burning skills.

A meadowlark. Ernie calls this a test bird with various stages of burning done on it.

Light and dark burns on the meadowlark. Shading, medium and dark burns, all effects that can be achieved with the burning tool can be seen.

this idea that the least amount of paint you put on a bird, the better off you are to obtain the effect you want without undercoating and hiding all your burning." For the moment, he seems to have forgotten the meadowlark and says, "I did a female cardinal not too long ago. This is a good example of what I'm trying to tell you. I burned it very lightly on the chest and put lacquer on it as an undercoat, and it looked just the way a female cardinal should look as far as the breast was concerned. But I heard someone say at a competition that the burned bird looked just like wood. For some reason that struck me as something maybe you shouldn't do."

Ernie was annoyed that someone questioned his technique. He returned to his studio and made two more female cardinals with burn lines. One he undercoated with a lacquer and washed with a mix of raw

umber and yellow ochre. The other he left unpainted. This one was for comparison.

"They looked exactly the same," he says, widening his eyes. "In other words, if you can get by with nothing, leave it that way."

Ernie is unable to resist another example. "Take a bobwhite quail. The edges of the secondary feathers are almost wood color or the color of raw wood. Now you could white it out with gesso and put yellow ochre and burnt umber washes and bring it back to the same wood color, but by doing that you fill in your burning detail that you want to retain to make it look feathery."

He concludes that the least steps done on a piece, the better it is. "If it looks good without anything on it, great. Try to keep it as simple as possible," he says reasonably.

He picks up the meadowlark and circles it with a pinky. "You'll retain the wood look and the lines burned in because what you put on afterward are washes with little undercoating and little opaqueness, and you end up looking at the finished job through transparent washes right down to the wood you started with."

Burning was not always a matter of taking today's lightweight pen handle and turning the knob on a heat-controlling rheostat box to allow for light lines and dark lines and a variety of shades. Carvers were burdened with burning tools hardly more sophisticated than soldering irons, and it's been said that Tan Brunet at one time used ice picks heated on his stove to score lines.

No one knows for sure when the first burn lines were made on the body of a wooden bird to define shaft and barb lines, the latter being those hairlike branches coming off the shaft of the feather. Barbs are one of the goals of the realists, for they are burning in 80, 150, even 220 barb lines per inch. Still, wood-burning tools have been around for several decades. Christmas and birthday gifts for kids now in their fifties made blackened illustrations in wood. It is likely, though, that a few carvers in North America tried them on their waterfowl in the 1960s. The birds most likely took on the texture of toothpicks, and carvers went back to making smooth birds and letting the paint brush create feather definition. But it was during the early 1970s that competitions exhibited birds with a great deal of burning, some finely rendered.

When Ernie started burning and required a range of heat settings, he experimented with a homemade rheostat. A simple wooden box, it had a socket on its top to accept a light bulb. Different wattages dictated the amount of heat in the pen. It is still in his studio, next to two newer, commercial models.

In the last few years, a few manufacturers of burning pens have offered an interesting assortment of tips. Some are skewed; some present long, thin tips. A multiline burner with razor-edge elements was in vogue among a few carvers. The design was rejected, however, because the lines it made were stiff-looking, too precise. Carvers want twists, curves, S-curves to their barb lines with barbs coming together at their ends or splitting apart randomly.

Still laying the final cellophane washes of burnt umber and ultramarine blue on his chickadee trio, he says for most of his burning he uses a tip called the

The first burning tool. A 100-watt light bulb and a light dimmer switch gave different degrees of heat.

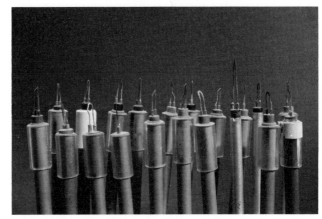

An assortment of different burning pens and tips used for different effects.

tight round, the one he designed. He goes over the whole bird first with a light burn after sanding it. "With a real low setting I do each feather quill and the barbs. Here, let me show you this point." There is a small-diameter turntable at his burning station with nineteen burning pens, each with a different tip, stuck into holes. The tight round point, its two prongs making it interchangeable with other tips, begins to end in a skew but projects out with narrow, parallel sides and ends in a rounded but flat tip.

He states evenly that he is pretty sure he designed the tip, then asked a pair of engineers who retail a burning kit called The Detailer to market it. Holding it in his hand as if ready to burn, he continues, "With this point, you can work perpendicular to your bird and actually backstroke." His fingers flick the pen along an invisible bird and return the pen to its original position. "It's quicker. I figure it's ten strokes with this point to three with a pointed one. That's because the tight round is sharpened on both the forward and leading edge so you can backstroke. With a sharp point you have to lift it up. Otherwise you'd be dragging it back to get to the next line. But you don't have to worry about that with the tight round.

"I timed myself on a chickadee using both a wedge-shaped tip and this guy here. Mine cut the time in half." He grins. "And it does a better job once you get used to using it."

Over the last few years a debate has been going on over the use of burning. One problem carvers have is where burning lines should be applied. Not all feather texture is the same. On the breast of a bird, feathers have a loose, sometimes vague and ambiguous look. Some carvers say they look coarse. These carvers usually make use of a disc-shaped grinding stone or any rotary stone with a hard edge. Another school of

carvers disdains the burning of wood, claiming it makes a poor surface for paint. But today, most carvers seem to favor both stoning *and* burning, the latter for feathers like tertials, secondaries and primaries. Ernie will stone in texture, but most of his feather definition is done with a burning pen.

After drawing in feather patterns and groups as he sees them on a bird, he sets the burning tool to zero. "It's just enough heat to make a dent in the wood but not enough to burn the wood," he explains. "I think the heat collapses the little fibers. I guess it's like steaming the lines in. And the lighter you burn, the tighter together you can burn." He pauses. "If you burn hot, the wood darkens, and you think some of that charcoal is taking up the width of the burn, and you think you're close, but you're not. So when you paint, you see a gap between each burn stroke. But you really want to burn as closely as you can." He picks up the meadowlark with the half-burned head. "You can see here how tight the burning is."

He continues on his burning strategy. "If I'm doing a quail, I go over the whole bird with a setting of 1 or 2 and shade each feather, still with the tight round. This seems to give the illusion of feathers sticking up in the air. I guess I burn while holding the pen at a 25-degree angle and work from the head on out. Then I'll go back over those lines with a hotter setting, dragging the tip with a decreasing pressure toward the feathers' edges. This will darken them. I call it shading. Then I'll switch to a pointed tip. I don't need a tight round now because I just set the new tip down and scorch an area darker to a real deep, deep brown." he says, drawing the words out.

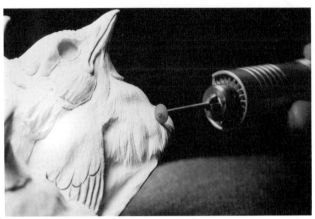

Not all feather texture is done with a burning pen. A disc-shaped grinding stone can give a coarser look.

The results of stoning under the rump on a woodcock, though burning was done over the grinding stone marks.

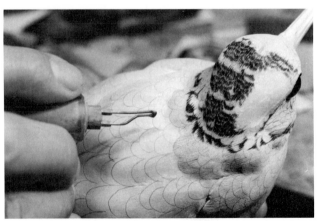

Most birds that Ernie does are first burned lightly with a tight round tip that he invented. Here he burns at a very low heat setting, a zero on some burning tools, on the back of a woodcock.

"Let's say we have a secondary feather on a quail. I'll burn light, then shade, then draw in lines defining where the light edges will be. A setting of 3 gives me a medium shade of brown. But on the leading edge we have a light burn and next to a preceding feather a shaded burn and a darker burn in the center part of the feather. After all that's done, I draw in dark marks and burn those in with a hot pen. Here, you can see them on the meadowlark." A finger pokes at the deep, dark markings on the chest and back of the bird.

"You could paint these spots in, but it's hard to get a real intense black with a paint brush. You have to hit them about ten times before you get it right. With a burning pen, you do it in one shot and get it just as dark as you want it. You have more control over what you do with a burning pen. With a brush, by the time the paint dries, the water has evaporated and it's not intense at all. It's too time-consuming."

He stares at the meadowlark on its cedar post for a few moments. "When you're done, you've actually passed over each individual feather about four times." He repeats the sequence. "Light burn, zero setting. Shading, number 2. Medium browns, number 3 or 4 setting. Dark with a 5 or 6 setting. But he warns, "Don't burn so dark that it produces smoke. If you're making smoke, you're burning too dark." He adds, "You're making charcoal and you're not getting a crisp look."

He picks up a paint brush but not a chickadee. He says that the bird must next be sealed. He uses lacquer and lacquer thinner, after having used an acrylic spray for years. Then he covers the bird with watered-down gesso. "If there is a white area, you gesso that

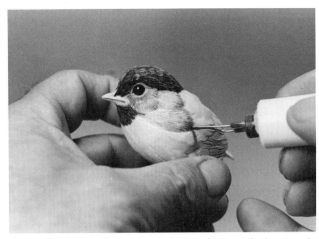

By bearing down hard at the end of a stroke, hairy feathers can be achieved, as on this baby chickadee. A tight round at a zero setting is used here.

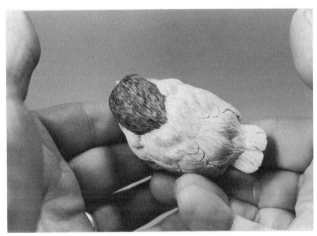

The back of the same chickadee. This has only two kinds of burns: one light for the body, one dark for the head.

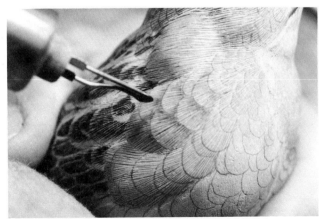

The second burn Ernie calls shading, with the burning tool turned up slightly higher. This is being done on the chest of a baby meadowlark. Photo courtesy of Wildfowl Carving and Collecting

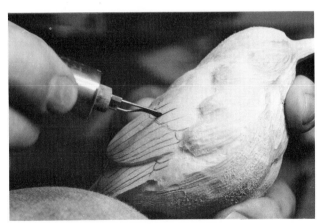

The tight round tip can also outline major feathers in the wing groups. Photo courtesy of Wildfowl Carving and Collecting

Dark lines are done with a skew tip with a high heat setting.

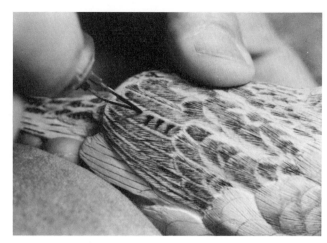

Feather bars can also be made with a sharp tip. Photo courtesy of Wildfowl Carving and Collecting.

With an even sharper tip, small dots can be made to outline feathers. This is a meadowlark being worked on. Photo courtesy of Wildfowl Carving and Collecting.

Some burning must be enhanced with a paint brush. This may mean adding some warm black to large areas of dark lines to give them a uniform color. Photo courtesy of Wildfowl Carving and Collecting.

The same sharp tip can make dark lines within the meadowlark's feathers. Ernie says this is like using a fine paint brush with dark paint on the tip. Photo courtesy of Wildfowl Carving and Collecting.

Comparing two immature meadowlarks shows the results of a light burn, shading, and patterns done with a sharp tip and high heat setting. Photo courtesy of Wildfowl Carving and Collecting.

The side of the finished baby meadowlark. Photo courtesy of Wildfowl Carving and Collecting.

A white-throated sparrow is another good bird for a intermediate burning project. There is a lot of variation of color on the back, he points out.

This woodcock is one of Ernie's favorite projects for burning. It takes many tones of browns and blacks.

The back of the same bird. Ernie says this is a good choice of a bird for a intermediate-level burning project. Photo courtesy of Wildfowl Carving and Collecting.

A closeup of a completely burned woodcock.

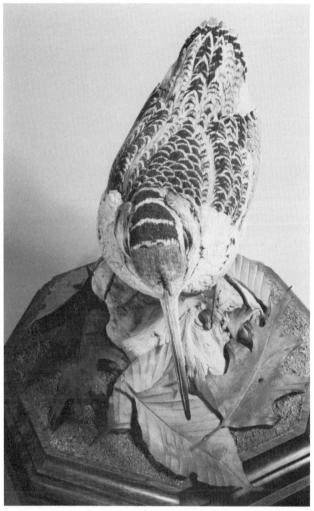

The back of the bird.

Another woodcock, showing the shading done on the breast.

out. Or if an area is yellow, you white that out. Or if you want a red for a cardinal, you have to put a white underneath. But for most birds I don't touch anything on the bird I got with the burning pen. That's the browns and blacks. So if it has to be a different tone from the earthy ones, you white it out and paint over that.

"Beige and blue make a nice gray," he says competently. "Put a blue wash on a nice brown burn, and you're going to end up with gray. If you want a vibrant brown, you put the brown washes on heavier. But I said that already, didn't I?" He laughs quietly.

"I guess I try to do as little on the bird as possible after burning it." He has a study skin of a bobwhite quail on his other table. He returns to his stool and says, "Look at all the browns and blacks on this bird." He spreads the back feathers with his thumbs. He turns the bird over and exposes its underside. "Under the chin would be whited out with my method. And all this on the chest between the dark and light marks, that would all be carefully whited out." As if he needs to further his point, he adds, "If you're doing a grouse, you white out the chest. And if you're doing one of these meadowlarks, you white out its chest, except where it's burned dark. Then you bring it up to the yellow. If you didn't do that the light burn and wood color would affect the yellow. You'd get a brownish yellow, not a true yellow.

"On my baby bluebirds, wherever there was a bright blue, I put down an undercoat of gesso. That way, the white enhanced the blue. Otherwise you'd get a grayish blue that wouldn't sparkle. On these chickadees, I have five coats of undercoat on the chests and one coat of gesso on the backs, plus the washes. And all the detailing was done with the burning pen."

Laying the skin that smells strongly of camphor on the other side of the turntable and resuming painting, he says, "I don't get into opaque painting. You blot out the wood effect. In fact, you can see the grain of the wood coming through the backs of these little guys. Sometimes the wood is soft, sometimes too hard. See those grain lines?" he says, poking a finger at the back of the chickadee to which he is applying a blue wash. "You get that when the wood's a little bit on the hard side. But you keep forging ahead. Sometimes a writer doesn't get the right paper to write on, does he?" He laughs.

Traditional and bird carvers talk about carving with the grain. They also talk about carving downhill. An analogy can be made with a telephone book. Open it to its middle and lay the two halves flat. Run a finger down the page edges of one half and there is no resistance. Reverse direction and the finger will quickly catch and open up the book to a new section. The same holds true for grain. Go against it or work uphill, and a section of the wood will start to tear away.

Carvers today have had remarkable success with carving the anatomy of tupelo birds while not worrying about keeping all the parts flowing with the grain. A particularly critical area is the bill, which rarely is positioned so that its grain is running in the same direction as the head. Even a curlew head, with its long, curling bill, is possible with tupelo.

Tupelo, or tupelo gum, is technically known as water tupelo and has been called sour gum, swamp tupelo, white gum, yellow and gray gum, and olive. It grows in a narrow belt about one hundred miles wide from southern Illinois through the Mississippi Valley to Texas and back along the coast up to Virginia. Growing best in swamps, it can attain heights of 100 feet and sometimes more, and diameters of 4 or 5 feet.

No one knows for sure how long tupelo has been floated as decoys, but carvers have tended to use available wood provided it was lightweight and reasonably workable and could be painted without problems of pitch or resins bleeding through the finish. Tupelo has merits in all three areas. Cajun carvers of southern Louisiana, those people who enjoy their French Canadian heritage, will go into the swamps to harvest it. This means bringing a boat and chainsaw into areas frequented by alligators and water moccasins. There they cut down these trees that grow in only a foot of water. However, it is only the bole or first 4 feet that is taken back. This has the best wood, as cabinetmakers have known for generations, usually with the best working properties. The rest is left to lay, partially submerged like the reptile residents of the swamps, until time and rot return the trees to the murky soil below the water.

For a long time Cajun carvers worked the wood green. This meant it did not go through either a forced or a natural process of water removal. For cabinetmakers, a 6 to 8 percent presence of water in wood is acceptable. In an unseasoned piece of wood, it might be 200 percent. Heavy, wet wood has a tendency to crack or check, owing to uneven shrinkage as the air comes into contact with inner layers of the tree too quickly.

"Tupelo burns real nice," Ernie says, "if you have a good piece. I have some light as a feather. Your burn-

One of Ernie's more interesting projects, a spruce grouse done in 1983.

A pair of ruffed grouse. In the collection of Andy and Sandy Andrews.

Some 8 to 10 miles of burning lines went on these birds.

The burned-in patterns on the tail.

ing pen will sink into it like it's a piece of butter. I wouldn't touch it."

He used a wood called jelutong for about half his

carving career. He criticizes it, saying, "It has pith holes and pores. Some of those you find where you don't expect to find them. Invariably they end up in an eye," he says, shaking his head slightly. "Basswood is all right, but it's fuzzy. It's hard to get nice and clean, although it burns O.K. I guess tupelo has the least amount of disadvantages. It's not fuzzy, it burns well, but," he seems unwilling to give unqualified acceptance, "it's inconsistent."

He looks again out the rear window of the studio. Maybe he's glimpsed a bird passing. "I once figured out how much burning I really do on a bird. On a pair of grouse, I estimated I had 8 to 10 miles of continuous lines. That was figuring on about a ¼-inch-long stroke. I guess it worked out on those two grouse that I had two million ¼-inch strokes, and laid end to end they would have been about 10 miles." He whistles a soft note.

"How long would it take to count to a million?" he asks quickly. "I burn about 5 strokes per second. Well, maybe 3 strokes per second. Three times 60 seconds, that's 180 strokes a minute. In an hour how many strokes do you have? Let's say you have 10,000 in an hour. Let's push it a bit. You have 100,000 strokes in a day. In ten days you have a million strokes, don't you? That was for one bird. For two birds, two million. What's a penny times two million? That's $20,000. That's what I got for a pair of grouse."

He inhales. "That owl of mine. I devoted sixteen hours a day for two weeks to burn it. What's fourteen times sixteen?" He shakes his head negatively. "I guess the owl had a good 15 or 20 miles of strokes on it. Let's see, is that a half a cent per line?"

Tiger of the Air

"The great horned owl was the most stressful time in eighteen years of carving," he says, hunching up his shoulders slightly and bringing his eyebrows together almost balefully. He lays his brush across the top of the plastic paint tray.

"It was just a lot of problems, and everybody else working for that championship was having problems. Tony Rudisill [a New Jersey carver] had his wings mounted too high or else they were too long on his red-shouldered hawk, and Bob Guge [of Illinois] was having problems with his legs and feet. The burrowing owls have hair growing out of their feet," Ernie explains, "and he didn't know how to handle that."

There are no reminders left in the studio of his eleven weeks of problems. There is no mounted owl collecting dust on a low shelf, though Ernie would tell you that tupelo dust from the weeks of carving still hides between pages of books and behind machinery and an oak china cabinet too cumbersome to move. Nor are there partially shaped-in-wood owl bodies pushed under the workbenches.

Eighteen to 25 inches long, with a wingspan of up to 60 inches, the great horned owl is widely dispersed throughout North America. Though nocturnal, it will hunt during the day in terrains ranging from mountains to deserts. Its ragged-edge feathers allow it, like all owls, to fly silently. A partial inventory of its prey includes rabbits, squirrels, rats, skunks, woodchucks, cats, ducks, geese, swans, turkeys, songbirds, perhaps even a game bird like a bobwhite quail.

Owls such as these will take their kill aloft to treetops. But some come to earth never to return to the air. Ernie's great horned owl began as a roadkill. "A roadkill is something that gets hit by a car," Ernie says. "It was from New Jersey, it had no damage, and it was in prime condition and at the right time of the year," he says, referring to its feather coloring. "It was fall, October, I think. It was just perfect," he says with a smile of satisfaction. "The taxidermist found only a bruise at the base of the skull, which probably severed the spinal cord."

He remembers that until the fall before the annual April contest called the World Championship Wildfowl Carving Competition, he did not know what to

Burning on the right wing of the great horned owl toward the end of the project.

The owl mount done from Ernie's sketches. The taxidermy work was done by Richard Smoker of Crisfield, Maryland. (See appendix for address.)

carve. The contest is probably the greatest challenge to a carver because of the number and quality of the entries. A ribbon taken home from this contest outcolors one taken from any other competition. A friend found the owl on Long Beach Island, New Jersey. "But you can't hang onto a bird like this without it being accounted for," in typical Muehlmatt fashion, he continues, "so I put it in the freezer and went to West Chester University where a friend arranged for a permit."

He relates how he needed both a federal and state permit before a taxidermist would touch it. The taxidermist was Richard Smoker of Crisfield, Maryland. "I brought the bird to him, and he worked the owl up according to my sketches pretty accurately and brought it to me in January. But before that, he took it to a taxidermist show in Baltimore and everybody liked it a lot."

The problems were to begin almost immediately. He needed wood to form the body. A solid block of wood would have started with dimensions of at least 10 inches on each side and approximately 24 inches long. Jelutong, the wood he was familiar with, is available in half that thickness at best. He tried clamping two 4-inch-thick by 10-inch-wide pieces together, but found voids between the faces of the wood. "I would have had to do some filling with Plastic Wood. It would have shown. It would have been bad," he admits as his lower lip droops slightly.

He tried another wood. This was tupelo gum, and for a second time he tried laminating wood. But the glue joint was not good, and the pieces split apart. Another piece of wood was not sufficiently seasoned—that too cracked as the stresses along the drying growth rings split the wood. Still another piece, this one measuring 8 by 8, was too hard. "So I finally got this guy in Wilmington [Delaware] to bring me a piece of tupelo. It was quite soft on one end, hard on the other," he says with some resignation, but shares that the Wilmington connection had warned him that a piece 24 inches long or longer will invariably have one end hard, the other soft. "That's what happened with the owl," he explains. "There's a short range where the wood is good. The head was almost too soft, the body was all right, but when I got to the tail, it was hard as a rock."

He walks toward his Foredom station, reaches down for a block of wood 4 inches on each side and 8 inches high, returns and puts it on the table. Its unevenly cut bottom rocks the wood for a moment. It is the color of straw, with fine and nearly uniform grain lines. "I used this jelutong for eight or ten years," Ernie recounts. "I had good success with it. It's nice, stable wood, and it burns well, but you can't get super-fine detail in it. But it's still a great wood. Jelutong has those sap pockets or whatever they are. They look like the tree grew around a blade of grass." There are density problems, and the splitting is not uncommon, he says, indicating that he has many pieces with splits in them. "And the trouble with those pores is they burn out and make a mess on the surface of the bird.

"Now why did I use jelutong? Well, I started out with basswood, no, sugar pine in the beginning, until Dan Brown [a close Maryland friend] told me to try a piece of basswood. That was until I went to a bird show out in San Diego. They all used this jelutong because they couldn't get basswood. I was one of the first in the East to use jelutong."

He makes an aside. "Somebody told me they used to use jelutong to deadload a boat coming back from somewhere. Junk.

"So how did tupelo work with that owl?" His smile helps answer the question. "As many times as I jiggled that thing in my lap and burned on it, ears sticking out, the sharp beak, the tail feathers down real low, nothing ever broke. I bumped it a good many times, and nothing ever broke. I think the bird would have been impossible to do in any other wood."

He exhales deeply, readying himself to continue, the paints and the chickadees neglected. "So the first time I got really serious about tupelo was because of this great horned owl. As I said before, I was familiar with it, though I debated whether I wanted to use it because I wasn't *that* familiar with it. But I needed that 10 by 10 by 24-inch block in one piece."

Ernie makes a revelation. He did not start carving

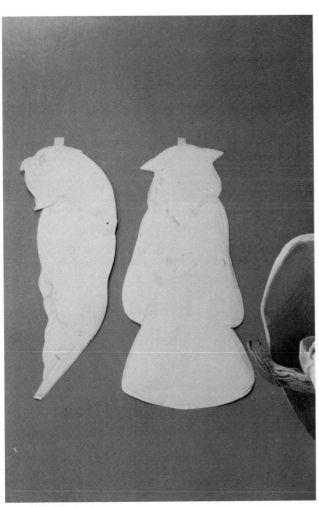

The top and side view patterns for the great horned owl.

The owl and bobwhite quail composition started with the owl's feet and its prey rather than with the body of the owl.

A closeup of the owl's legs and feet and the dead bobwhite quail.

A closeup of the claws clutching the dead quail.

The bobwhite quail after burning.

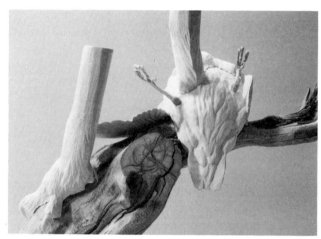

The back view of the quail and owl legs.

The mounted quail for comparison.

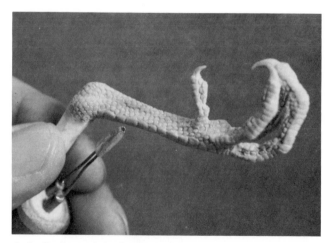

A detail of one of the dead quail's feet. Ernie put what he calls an adaptor on the end of a burning pen tip to make the scales. These feet, like the rest of the composition, were made from tupelo.

the body until he had carved both of the legs for the owl and its prey, a bobwhite quail. While the owl was still in a square block of tupelo, a carved quail lay draped over a thick branch. The owl's foot and talons that clutched it were carved, not separately, but as part of the body and rose up like a stump. The other foot clutched the branch tightly and that, too, rose up as a leg waiting for a body.

"The choice for the species of dead bird was Smoker's idea. Originally, I wanted a woodcock, but that long, straight bill wouldn't have fit the design. But anyway, after two attempted dead quail I got something I was fairly pleased with. Then I worked on the other leg and had many, many problems," he says with a short sigh. "Why did I have so many problems?" he asks himself as if trying to jog free an unpleasant memory. "I just didn't know where else to start from. The main thing was to get the legs the right distance apart."

He admits that there was a step before that. It was finding the wood for the owl to stand on. "It was more interesting on the branch than on a flat tree stump." He adds, reflectively, "I liked it at different heights. It flowed better one leg up, one leg down. And that affected the wing levels, compensating for balance," he says, rocking the jelutong block in front of him with the tip of a forefinger.

"I spent a week down below," meaning the first floor of the building, "trying to find the wood to sit the owl on. There must be two thousand pieces of wood there," he muses. "And what I ended up with I carved 50 percent anyway to make it fit the position of the feet and for the dead quail to drape over."

He picks up a paint brush and waves it gently. "You know, I didn't even know if owls eat quail. The quail is basically a daytime feeder, and the owl is a nocturnal bird. Where would an owl find a quail at night? But they do eat quail, pheasants, skunks."

The quail itself, its head drooping in death, its wings cupped upward, offered more problems. "I never realized carving a bird upside down would be so difficult. It was like doing a portrait of somebody standing on his head. You had to work on it as you saw it." He adds, "You see, I'm used to working on birds in a certain sequence from the head down the back to the wing coverts and out the wings, the rump, the tail. This way," he says, "I was working on the belly first. You know what I mean?"

Fitting the quail and other foot to the branch created new problems to overcome. "It was a job fitting every-

thing to the driftwood." He describes any natural wood as if it were found on a beach, though most of his wood never felt a tide and some, coming from the deserts, rarely felt water. "I used a lot of carbon paper between the dead bird and the other leg and the branch. You tap the wood and see where the carbon paper leaves a mark. Then you carve that away. Boy, did that take time."

He recalls that at first he had the legs too far apart, an inch too far. The quail, too, was too high above the wood when that distance was lessened. "So I had to chop down on my driftwood and on the body of the quail. I guess I brought the driftwood down ¾ inch and the body of the quail down ¼ inch."

When he did get around to working on the body, he started to carve it, but without a head. "I had an idea I

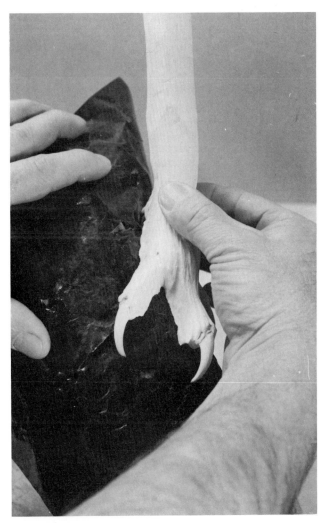

To fit the owl's feet to the limb, carbon paper had to be put between each foot and branch. The marks left by the carbon paper were ground away until the foot fit almost perfectly.

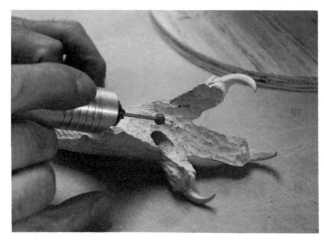

Here Ernie demonstrates carving away wood from under one of the feet.

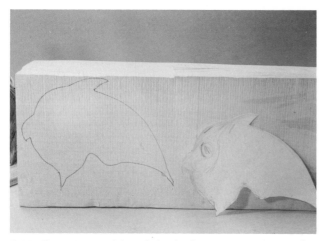

Originally, Ernie wanted the owl's head to be a separate component, but he abandoned that idea because of the joint showing.

The carved owl's face before burning.

was going to carve the body without the head, you know, carve the head separately and fit it to the body. But I got the body fairly well carved without the head and I said 'How the hell am I going to do this so that they fit together properly?' I guess I thought it would be easy to handle just the head in my hands because the body is so big. I didn't think I could handle what ended up as an 18-inch-long piece of wood. I was even going to do the tail separately, but I abandoned that idea."

He sighs again. "I guess it worked out better that I did it in one piece except when I got burning the tail topside and underside. I had to hang onto it and not knock off the ears or beak." His voice has taken on a tone of exasperation.

"So I started out with the head, the eyes, the beak — thinking if you get the head right, you got 90 percent of it. But for some reason, it didn't look right. I kept looking at it every morning until I took some measurements and found that the eyes and face weren't sunk in far enough." He was fortunate. "When I took more measurements, I found I still had more wood in the head to reset the eyes and redo the bill." He laments that it meant recarving the face, bringing the plane of it back ¼ inch.

"Anyway, the head was nice to work with. It was soft. But the rump and tail were hard and rubbery even working with a 1¼-inch diameter carbide cutter on my stationary motor. It was a hell of a job."

Absently, he wipes a finger across his tabletop, perhaps searching for tupelo particles. But the visible owl dust has been gone for a year. "By that time, I had sawdust in every hole in my body. Maybe I had an allergic reaction to the sawdust, or a cold, but for a couple of weeks I had trouble breathing. It felt like I had the flu, but I kept pushing on until I dragged myself out every morning. *Finally* things started looking up because it burned nicely." Still, not everything else went that well. "Another problem was that the owl weighed by that time 12 pounds. Just holding onto it while burning, flipping it around twelve hours a day, wore me out. Your hands and arms get tired. Then if the phone rang, I had to set the bird down gently."

He reaches out and rotates the birds' turntable a few degrees counterclockwise, looking at the chickadees on it. Is he weighing songbirds against owls? The great horned owl may weigh 250 times more than a black-capped chickadee.

He pauses to resume painting one of the chickadees, lifting it from the turntable by the holding fixture he

The owl's body from the underside, also prior to burning.

The flat area is where the left wing will be screwed into place. A carved scapular, which will slide into the hollow area, will cover the screws.

To make the scapulars, Ernie made clay models first. The clay is on the left; the wooden scapular is on the right. The pegs protruding will hold it in place without screws or glue.

has made with a steel clip and stick. He swirls his brush around in the brown wash to reduce the gray of its back. "Oh, yes, the wings," he says abstractly. "One wing was super wood, the other, hard as a rock." He did not have a bandsaw with an exposed blade big enough to shape the wings. The wings were nearly 12 inches across. After using a friend's machine, he had to contend with what he describes as a clamshell look. After getting the outside curvature, leaving about an inch of wood for the thickness, a Forestner bit took out circles of wood on the insides of the wings, leaving a hollow.

A new problem managed to arise. How was he to fit these manteling wings, and the scapulars, which are the shoulder feathers of a bird and look like epaulets, to the body? Tracing paper was again used, as was clay. Ernie says that after using number 10 wood screws to secure the wings, he made the scapulars out of clay and fit them to the body. These were his models. With the tracing paper between the body and wings and the roughly shaped wooden scapulars, he was able to replay the technique he used with the feet and branch. Rapping the scapulars with a hammer left a mark on their undersides wherever the fit was not flush. He beams a smile. "It was a perfect fit. There's no filler. It's wood to wood. But I had to fit feather breaks in the seams to minimize that line where two pieces of wood join." He had succeeded in designing an owl with wings that could be removed for transport and replaced on arrival.

He relates a general, disquieting frustration. "Many nights I would go home frustrated with the owl and thinking, 'I'm never going to make it to the competition.'" Now he compares the experience to childbirth pains. "Women don't remember that pain after the baby is born."

The back of the owl without the wings and scapulars.

The wings have been detailed and the scapulars fit fairly well.

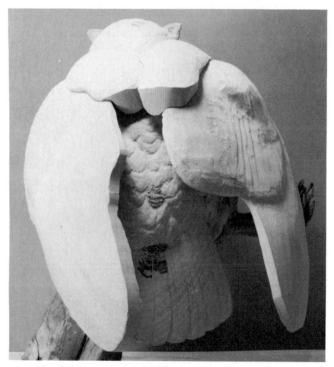

The rough-carved wings and scapulars in place.

Ernie thought it would be interesting to have the one wing of the dead bird cutting into the soft feathers of the owl's leg. The overlapping feathers were made from Tuf Carv, a wood filler.

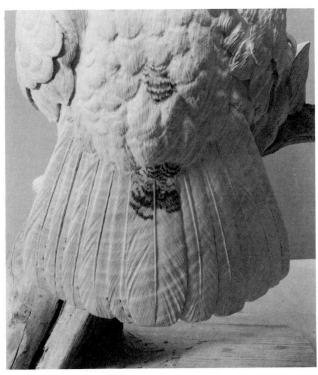

Some trial burning on the owl's tail. Note the grain of the tupelo, which made carving this area very difficult.

The completely burned owl and quail without paint.

The burned face of the owl.

A closeup of the tail showing its intricate feather design.

The owl's right side.

After burning on the bird, a new worry manifested itself. He began to question the color of the mounted bird. "I thought I had a good color on my mount. But then you get to wondering if it was a freak with wrong colors, which you run into. I remember an owl I did for a show once that was a hybrid. So I didn't know if my great horned owl was typically colored." A bird encyclopedia offered an answer. The colors described in the text fit those of the mount, adding that this owl's color darkened when it was found residing further north on the continent, lightened as it made its home south.

"I still wasn't finished after piecing everything together and figuring out how to paint it. I had to figure out what color the eyes are. You can't tell from a dead bird." He pauses to think. "I guess they're straw-colored." He called six taxidermist supply companies to make orders. "I would get too small a pupil, too large a pupil. But I wanted an owl with a large pupil to show that it was a nighttime owl. I had a terrible time finding owl eyes with large pupils. Then some were too flat, some the wrong color. It was enough to drive you crazy. Without the right eyes, you just don't have the right look about it."

Its left side.

The back.

He continues, his shoulders drooping a bit. "Finally, I got a name from New York City. It was in *How to Carve Wildfowl*. It turns out he's the oldest dealer of glass eyes in the United Sates. So I ordered three pair in case I dropped some. I literally spent about $200 on eyes. But when they came in, they were gorgeous." He smiles. "There was no epoxy on those lids. They're all wood. It was a tight fit. Hairy. I had to slide the eyes from the lower lids up."

Picking up a chickadee and the brush, Ernie says, "The painting was very easy. I did that in a couple of days with a big brush. I went to one area and slopped the paint on. Tupelo is a lot easier to paint. Water and acrylics kind of flow. The woods sucks up water. So you get a nice blending of color. It's like painting wet on wet. But you wouldn't do that for little birds like these chickadees."

He retreats back to the painting and has to ask himself what he had just said. "Oh, yeah. Tupelo just doesn't repel water. It bleeds into the wood, so you don't get a hard line." He notes that his owl had a great deal of white, burnt sienna and grays in its coloration.

As the body took on its millions of burn lines, Ernie wondered what he should add to the base. Would he

The painted left side.

The painted back of the owl.

The front of the owl. Below it is a low-growing rhododendron plant ready to bloom.

have an earth composition made of synthetic materials, or would he put the branch on a walnut base without habitat? He went with the earth and added a low-growing rhododendron plant. Earlier he had argued with himself that a flower or plant would detract from the design of the owl and quail.

"There's so much burnt sienna, reddish tones in the chest parts, that it needed something to counterbalance that mass of color in the owl. So I used the green of the rhododendron to pull it all together." He says he shaped the leaves from tupelo, making them paper-thin in places. "You could almost see through them," he remembers.

The use of rhododendron was based on a physical presence of the plant. Outside his building are tall-growing rhododendron bushes. Ernie explains, "I picked the model for it right outside here in, oh, I guess it was early April. It was just the way you saw it under the owl, a rhododendron with a bud coming out. In another month or two, it would be in bloom."

He remembers that someone challenged his use of such a low plant. "Somebody came up here and said it wouldn't grow that short out of the ground. It wouldn't have those big leaves when it's only 3 inches high. I said, 'You want to bet?' We went outside and found hundreds of them with huge leaves and only that tall. What happens is that a long branch sags, dips

A baby great horned owl Ernie found outside his house one morning.

into the soil, and lays there a couple of years in rotten leaves. It makes its own roots. You can actually cut it away from the mother plant and it will continue to grow."

Ernie feels he faced one more ordeal. "I even had problems putting the bird into the show." He confesses, "I don't like when you enter a show and you have to go from the front door to the table to get the bird out of the box and onto the table. And then friends and others gather around and watch, and it's difficult setting it up, and they're going 'ooh' and 'aah.' It would have been nicer if I could have set up the owl all by myself. I had to be so careful unpacking it."

The dog that has taken its 4½ square feet of floor space for a part of the day rises and shakes itself. "Beanie wants to play ball," Ernie says. But the dog will have to find its own ball and company, for Ernie continues to lay washes of color on the chickadees.

His ironic laugh returns. "Well, you know I didn't win." The owl and quail placed third in the competition, behind Larry Barth's snowy owl and Bonapart gull and Anthony Rudisill's red-shouldered hawk and rabbit. Twenty thousand dollars went to Barth, a purchase prize; $1,000 went to Rudisill; and $500 was set aside for Ernie, and he was allowed to take the owl home.

Ernie has opinions on judges, and he himself has judged a great number of competitions. "No matter how fair a judge is, he still has his favorites. And if he knows somebody and two birds are alike in quality and accuracy, he's going to go for the guy he knows. But who else can you get?" He says this seriously. "Art critics, ornithologists, they're so picky. They say this color is not right or they count feathers. But I know more about a great horned owl than a lot of ornithologists. When you pick apart each feather as I did, you've got to know the bird. Years from now someone will pluck a feather out of a great horned owl and I'll be able to tell you it came from that owl!" He laughs.

"You know, I would rather see a prize of $5,000 and you keep your piece. Then you wouldn't feel obligated to knock your socks off and take months and months to do what everybody thinks has to be a bird that's worth $20,000. Or have a big trophy. I think the prize money causes a lot of hard feelings."

He says it did not really matter that he didn't take first place. The results were enough. The challenge and the look of the bird and its prey greatly pleased him. "The dead quail is totally limp. I tried to get that into her. She's a hen, her head is stretched out, her legs are limp. She's beautiful in her own lifeless way. I guess relaxed. There's no rigor mortise that's set in," he says, as if he were speaking of a freshly killed bird. "She's beautiful in her looseness, and the owl is tense in contrast."

He dips the paint brush into his burnt umber wash. "I gave that owl a defiant look, as if to say, 'This is my kill. Don't come near me.' So the owl has his dinner under his foot and this is the look he gives you. I could have had the owl looking at its dinner or looking off someplace. But the owl knows you're there. That makes you part of the story. It worked better that way. Does this make any sense?" Another laugh, deeper this time.

Magic Moments

"A little more brown wash on this guy," Ernie says to himself, tapping the excess paint off the brush as he continues to work on one of the immature chickadees. He had not read that nearly 150 years ago naturalist Henry David Thoreau had listed among his most significant experiences the brief perching of a bird on his shoulder. Nor had Ernie known that only a decade or so earlier wildfowl artist Grainger McKoy walked into a group of bobwhite quail, resulting in a flurry of wings rising up almost into his face. What came of this was his covey of quail sculpture, thirteen birds in the act of escaping the bounds of the earth. But Ernie has had his own encounters.

"I was up in Canada with Jim Sprankle [a Maryland waterfowl carver] a couple of years ago," he explains, not stopping the painting, "and we were walking through the woods, and I stopped for a minute. I turned my head and two feet away from me, looking right at me, was a rose-breasted grosbeak. That was something you don't see too often."

Placing the chickadee in front of the hairdryer, he relates another chance meeting. His studio, before he moved into his present one, was a small, one-level building next to a pond. It is now a shop where his wife sells Christmas and other seasonal gifts, many of the items relating to wildfowl. He was cleaning his brushes in the pond water in the fading light of the evening. "As I was stooped over, I saw in the corner of my eye a little woodcock looking at me, and I was looking at him. That was neat. He didn't know what to do. After ten seconds, he chickened out and took off."

Ernie is caught up with stories of close encounters with wildfowl. "I was walking through those thick pine trees out behind my house and I heard some crows making a racket. About six feet from me was this great horned owl with his tigerlike face. It was an awesome sight.

"I guess I have that in the owl piece. You come upon him in the woods, and he's looking straight at you, and he's saying, 'This is my dinner and you're not going to get it.' Five seconds later, maybe, he'd see this as too tight a spot to be in and he'd fly off."

He removes another chickadee from its perch and fills his brush with the gray wash. He creases his forehead slightly in thought. "Maybe this is why people are so interested in bird carving. When do we ever get

A mourning dove in a position where it first sees a human.

A magic moment suggests the first moment of contact with a stranger.

a chance to come within arm's length of a bird other than a mounted one? The way to present a carved bird is as if you're walking through the woods and you're within three feet of a bird and the instant the bird sees you and you see the bird—it may be only a split second—it zooms off. That should be the bird carving, that instant where each recognizes the other. That's what I try to put into my carvings, that magic moment."

Relaxing his brush hand on the table, he says, "Most of my birds are looking at the guy who's looking at them. I think that's what people like. It includes you in the bird carving. You're part of it. If you weren't there, what would the bird be looking at?" His voice rises slightly, then lowers. "You take these little chickadees, all lined up. Every one of them is looking at you. If I had them looking at each other, you'd be out of the picture."

Has this robin just noticed a person standing near it?

A pair of semipalmated plovers, possibly caught by surprise.

Three woodcocks sunning themselves that have just been stumbled upon by someone walking through the woods.

He lists other pieces he has done. There were a pair of ruffed grouse resting in forest leaves. These, too, were at that moment of realization that they were not alone. Three woodcocks Ernie describes as sunning themselves were also at that small moment of awareness that someone was watching them. "It's only a moment before they're all gone. So I like to arrange my pieces so the viewer is part of the carving."

Ernie is aware, though, that not all carvers arrange their birds in moments of meeting man. He mentions carving compositions in which birds look at each, or are feeding off the ground, or are in flight. It is this last phenomenon, one that has birds suspended on steel feathers attached to pieces of habitat, that Ernie finds particularly discomforting.

"With something exploding off the ground and flying away, you end up wondering when they're going to finish. It's not the moment in time before they burst away." His early art training apparently comes back to him when he says that a good wildlife artist would not put his deer in midair as it leaps a fallen tree. It would be ready to jump, or it would be at the end of its jump. A land animal in midair, Ernie says, leaves the viewer with a feeling of discomfort.

"A magic moment can last for a long time, so you want to prolong the birds staying where they are. That's what you can put in your living room, isn't that so?" But Ernie begins to wonder if his thinking is valid. "Haven't these principles been established a long time ago?" He seems to be debating with himself when he says, "Experimentation put the bird into flight, but today there's more interest in a quiet pose."

He straightens up in his stool. "Yes. Take *The Kiss* by Rodin. You could sit and look at that for hours. It's peaceful." His tone becomes more strident. "*The Pieta.* It's great. There's no Olympic jumper in midair to tire you out. That makes sense, doesn't it?

"And keep it simple," Ernie adds axiomatically. "Boy, I see this in a lot of competitions. Some guys bring in a piece with all kinds of habitat and insects, and the bird is going through all kinds of motions. The simpler you make the piece—wings in, a quiet position—the less the judges have to pick apart. Tan Brunet always says this. But new carvers think if the bird is doing active things, they're going to win a prize. If it was harder to do, they should get points for difficulty, they'll tell you. But if you put a wing up and the judges see something wrong, you've lost. Nobody knows what's going on underneath a wing," he counters. "So keep it that way." He nods to himself.

"So what do we have so far? We have a quiet look and a magic moment. I guess I also give the birds an individual look." He lets out a short burst of laughter. "I get accused of doing Walt Disney-looking birds, chipmunky-looking birds, cheeky birds, I guess they are," he says quietly. "Well, I do accent the puffiness of the cheeks and try to give them a pleasant expression. But I don't know how that came about. It's just the way I see it. Right or wrong, that's the way I see it.

"But I try to feel what a chickadee would feel like. I do baby birds, so I puff up my cheeks and ask myself what would I be doing if I were a baby bird sitting on that branch?" He uses the end of the paint brush as a pointer. "For that matter, how does a quail or a woodcock feel? The woodcock feels scrunched up, pudgy with no neck, a long bill and very short legs. It's different from another bird that struts around, isn't it?"

He returns to the cheeky birds. "It's really what people like. Yeah, and I'm conscious of doing it. But I don't really know whether I like it or not," he says in an even voice. "But people must like it because they buy it, don't they?" He lowers his voice slightly, and, as if he needs to change this topic, he says, "I think this bird is a little bit gray. I'll tone it down, warm it up with the burnt umber wash."

He tests the wash on what he describes as a spot not too obvious and decides he will coat the entire bird with the less-than-cellophane-thin paint.

"Yeah, I think I have a feel for baby birds." But he complains how difficult it is to find the reference material needed. And for him that means photos and preserved skins. For one grouping of baby bluebirds, color photos were made available to him. He explains that a friend (he calls him a bluebird expert) took the pictures at a nesting area in Maryland for this species. Park rangers there can actually take immature birds out of their nests. But even with references available, Ernie admits, "Fifty percent of the baby birds I do are out of my imagination. I did some baby cardinals, and they were completely out of my head."

Ernie explains how he plausibly arrives at a bird he has never seen. "At three weeks old, baby birds are as big as the adult bird, and the color is usually like the female of the species. And they have that fleshy part at the sides of the beak that recedes and hardens as the bird gets older." He circles the face of a baby chickadee with his pinky as he explains. "That's so they can open their mouths real wide. It's kind of rubbery, stretchy material, like lips."

There are other features. "The little tail is quite

A baby bluebird taken out of its nest by a park ranger. Photos of baby birds are scarce.

short, only about half an inch long. The primaries are not yet in; the secondaries are short; but other than that, the feet are the same at three weeks. Some babies are bigger than the adult because they feed a lot and don't have to move around so much.

"At three weeks they start to fly and tighten up and slim down. Their muscles get in tune, the tail grows, the wings grow and they take on the male or female markings or colors. On these chickadees, the sexes are alike. They have the same colors."

He says, though, that these growing trends are not the same for all birds. "Some birds take two years to take on the colors of the adult birds. Take seagulls. They're brown and gray and mottled, and it takes that long before they get the adult colors. But with songbirds, it's usually three weeks."

He believes he can comfortably carve a baby songbird without seeing one. "Who really knows what some of these babies look like? You don't really know

A baby wood thrush. Note the stubby tail.

Ernie makes his baby birds pudgy. Also note the short primaries.

A back view of the titmouse.

He also makes the immature birds pouty looking.

Ernie will also give his baby birds an awkward stance when he can.

Ernie likes to give a baby bird a lost or forlorn look, as he did on this baby tufted titmouse.

Ernie says this baby robin is screaming for worms.

Another meadowlark standing up, with the mother coming closer. At three weeks the feet on a baby bird are as big as they will get, Ernie says.

A baby meadowlark, patiently waiting on a fencepost for the mother to return with food. Photo courtesy of Wildfowl Carving and Collecting.

until you pick one out of the nest and hold it in your hand."

But there *is* an ideal time to see the baby, he says. It is that very time when the bird leaves the nest only to reappear as an adult. "You might get a fleeting glimpse of a baby in the wild, but not very often. It's so hard to find them. They're more secretive at that age. In fact, the mother herds them away from people. So they're not likely to come to your feeder at three weeks."

He recalls a cardinal nest visible from one of the studio windows. He watched them every day and planned to get photos when they were ready to leave the nest. "Before that, there's a lot of skin and pin feathers on them and they have these skinny necks. They're not very attractive. Two weeks went by and I waited to get them a day or two before they left the nest. But how do you really anticipate that? I noticed

A baby kildeer. In the collection of Andy and Sandy Andrews.

A baby chickadee waiting for its mother.

The back of the bird.

This baby cardinal has a typically pouty look with its down-turned lips. Ernie says this bird was done from imagination.

that they had some feathers and I thought they were ready to leave. I thought I'd give them one more day and take some pictures, even if I had to pick them out of the nest. The next day they were gone." He laughs, "Evidently, the mother took them out into the woods and fed them. But when they come back, they're just like the rest of them." He straightens up in his seat. "I guess the cardinals I did were right, because I sold them right away."

He feels a need to do more with his baby birds. He describes his intent as one of "loosening up." He says, "I want to do different poses for my babies. I want to get them more animated and twisted, have them in more interesting positions."

He had seen a painter's presentation of a Hungarian partridge, wings back, dusting itself. "It was great," Ernie says characteristically. "But I was kind of

The body of the baby cardinal was carved to fit its base, which is a rock.

Like the great horned owl's feet, the bottom of the baby cardinal was fitted to its rock with the aid of carbon paper.

annoyed with myself when I saw that. I've been doing the same thing over and over, the same old conservative poses. I want to do something a little bit different."

In spite of what he sees as a shortcoming, he calls his birds individuals, though he isn't certain how that term applies to wildfowl. He does see individuality in a friend's carvings. Robert Guge is more than twenty years younger than Ernie and lives in a town twenty miles outside the boundaries of Chicago. Guge too carves primarily songbirds, and, like Ernie, won two Best-in-World titles with miniature compositions. Once was in 1984 when Ernie was accepting Best in World for somewhat larger birds. "Guge does a tree sparrow that's real neat," Ernie says. "You know it's cold because the bird is all puffed up, and the toes are tucked in, and his head is turned around to the side, and even the cheeks are puffed up. It's telling you the bird is trying to keep warm. The body is fluffed up against the cold, so you know it's wintertime. There's your story right there," he concludes. He brings the logic one step further. "If you do a nice sleek bird that's not puffed up and it's summertime, it's not telling you anything."

Something reminds him of the lifesize snowy owl and its prey, a Bonapart gull, that Pennsylvania carver Larry Barth brought to the 1985 World Championships, leaving it and taking home a Best-in-World title and $20,000. "There was a story," Ernie says with an overt admiration. "You could feel the wind in that piece, and the sea coast, the coldness." He stops painting as if for emphasis. "Sometimes these things happen in a composition. Sometimes they never happen. It's like a magic moment. For some people those never happen."

He resumes painting. "The worst problem I have with designing pieces is worrying about making a living. I'd like to take the time to do things with preliminary sketches, develop a theme for each piece like my quail piece or owl. But you don't have time to do that. You go to a show and somebody gives you an order for, say, chickadees, and you do a nice job, but you can't put a lot of thought into it." He explains that for the trio of baby chickadees, he has put in five days of shaping, burning, and painting. "I might have put in three weeks on them, spending time to make them more interesting, maybe have one slipping off balance. Make another annoyed by his buddy sitting next to him, maybe one with the wings out a bit. But," and his pause is an ellipsis, "you have to make a living," he adds quietly.

Robert Bateman is not the only artist to whom Ernie relates. "Did I mention Don Briddell's comments on carving?" He has not, nor does he explain that Briddell generates a number of articles relating to the carving of birds. "Briddell says that other art forms ask questions, while what we do leaves nothing to speculate about, except maybe how a wooden feather ends up looking like a real feather. And then he talks about the profit motive, and that people want a good bird, but they want to argue about prices. And how many ribbons has it won? I've heard that before. And then someone comes to your table and wants a bird exactly like the one that has a 'sold' sticker on it. And you take the competitions. There you have people measuring bill sizes. So where's the art?"

He does not deny that he has profited with having done large numbers of birds bought by people who may not have been as discriminating as he would have liked them to be. Nor does he doubt that he has carved more chickadees than any other person shaping wood. At least three thousand, he says. As if to support his claim, he explains that he would do ten chickadees per day when he started carving, though he calls them stylized, a term carvers use to describe birds lacking detailed texture and a paint application that suggests more than copies feather patterns and colors. The ten he made in those early years would be carved by noontime and painted in the afternoon. He makes a quick calculation that ten birds times six working days equals sixty birds per week. After only a year, he realizes, three thousand birds would be made.

"That's a lot of chickadees," he says. "I'd sell them for $3 or $4 apiece. Now I do only thirty or forty birds a year, and they're not all chickadees, obviously. But I was cranking them out, wasn't I?" he laughs mischievously.

"So I guess that's why I do songbirds. They're small and easy for me to do, and something I thought people would buy, and I know something about songbirds. The guys who do waterfowl are usually hunters. I never hunted a duck in my life," Ernie admits dryly.

He works silently for an amount of time made more uncomfortable by the low, monotone hum of the hairdryer that is suddenly audible. Finally, he clears his throat and says, "So what have I covered here? You try to get some emotion into the piece, some feeling. Put some thought into planning a piece and try to tell some kind of story, no matter how weak you may think it is. That's better than having the birds just sitting there. You take these three little chickadees, all lined up. Every one of them is looking at you. If I had them looking at each other, you'd be out of the picture." He looks thoughtfully at the branch with two of the three birds still looking out into space. "I like to think that when you're looking at it, you're the mother bird. You're coming up with a nice, juicy morsel, and the babies are looking at you. I guess it's basically designing the piece so it does something when you're looking at it."

He puts the chickadee that is getting warmed up with a transparent wash of brownish paint in front of the hairdryer. He may have seen something new in the composition. He says, "Look at that bird there on the branch. He looks cocky bracing himself. You can almost feel a little bit of tension there, can't you?"

Heaven, Earth, and Man

Two great horned owls nest in a Norway spruce near Ernie's house. The crows that harass them mornings and evenings are the daily reminder that they are there. Perhaps they remind Ernie as well of the two months of shaping, the two weeks of burning 15 miles of lines on the body, the wood that went bad.

"There was an overall flow to the piece," he says of the carved owl and its quail. "The first place you would look would be in the owl's eyes, then out one wing, down its tail, up the other wing, and back to the face. There was nothing there that would throw your eye out of the composition."

His explanation for the design that holds the eye is the circle. "You had the circle of the mask of the face and the eyes," he says making small arcs with the paint brush, the chickadees long overdue for a wash. The owl has a beard or bib. That's a circle. The dead quail had a lot of curves. Everything flowed around and around." He says that one wing of the quail lifted up and seemed to become part of the feathers of one owl leg. "There's a whole bunch of circles or ovals with nothing to throw your eye off the piece.

"I think the piece had a nice design. If the wings had been out further or too high, or if the head had been to one side, that would have made for a bad design, one with a conflict in it," he adds. His original idea was to have a woodcock, but the taxidermist chose the quail. He accepts now that the woodcock would not have been as effective. "The bigger head, the long, straight bill wouldn't have fit the design. Even the hooked bill of the quail had a circular design. A long bill would have shot your eye away."

He summarizes. "Your eye kept circling around the piece. The circular mask of the face, the manteling position of the wings, the dead bobwhite quail itself, the one wing out, all continued the circular motion. Even the rhododendron was a starburst circle," he says. At first he wanted no habitat, worrying that even stones or leaves would bring the eye away from the birds. "But even with the plant, there was nothing to lead your eye away. It kept you entertained. It made your eyes laugh." He pauses to stir his wash, though he does not continue painting. "These are the same principles we learned in advertising school."

He attended advertising and art school thirty-five years before he started the great horned owl. There he learned that page layout is not arbitrary but is based on principles of design and composition. They may not require circles, but whatever was put on the page had to take control of the eyes. "If you open to a page of advertising, you have something there to get your attention – a picture, bold lettering. Then once it gets your attention, it should subtly lead you into something else. From there to something less interesting. Then maybe it would lead you around to the name of the company again. But in no way should it allow you to become bored. Nor would a good page dare have an arrow at the bottom of the page, because then you'd have a tendency to turn the page over." He pauses, then says, "It's the same with bird carving."

His next statement is not about birds but about a soda bottle. "The old Coke bottle had a dynamite design, an almost sensual design. It looked like a woman's body. That's why you can sometimes be fooled into thinking a product is good when it may not be. Take the Studebaker. It was a good design but a lousy car."

Ernie moves to architecture and one of its leading American innovators of the organic house that functioned as part of its natural surroundings. "Frank Lloyd Wright built a pretty picture. It was like a giant flower arrangement. I don't think he sat down and designed a house without looking at where it was going." Ernie makes the transition back to birds. He says he begins not with a bird but with its base and designs the bird or birds to fit that. The base for the great horned owl required days of sorting through pieces of wood the right size but few the right shape for the owl and quail. Over two thousand pieces of

wood, he believes, are in a room below his studio. As it turned out, he reshaped much of the wood to allow the quail to drape over it without a gap. He did the same for his *Needles, Feathers, and Bone* composition of bobwhite quail in a desert setting. The skull was carved before the birds. "If I had carved and painted five quail and said, 'Where am I going to put them?' they wouldn't have fit right. The base should always come first in your mind."

He has put the three chickadees back on their branches. "I started with the base first, a nice twisty piece of wood, and arranged the birds one at a time," he says. The branch forks into two branches that seem partially to encircle the three birds. He describes the branches as "kinks that lead your eye around," though he had to piece together some of the wood with pins and a wood filler. The filler then had to be painted the color of the original wood.

He says that, like the owl, his chickadees form a nice, pleasing arrangement, owing in part to the choice of three birds. "An uneven number works out better than an even number." At first he claims not to know why. But he says, "In flower arrangements, we always used an uneven number of three, five, or seven flowers. Even numbers are too balanced. And if you do have only two birds, you'd need something else to balance the composition: a little swatch of color, or a stone, or a flower as your third component. I think your eye bounces back and forth between two birds with no flow. A pair of birds is worse than one bird for arranging."

Of the single bird, he says, "You can get the finest-looking bird, but stand it still on a piece of driftwood

Developing a central line with the wood, a line to the left and one to the right, all adapted from the principles of Japanese flower arranging.

Though there are 8 chickadees in this composition, 7 of them are young birds. The one in front is the mother. In the collection of Andy and Sandy Andrews.

Developing an arrangement of bird and base, using the S-curve of the wood.

A piece of ghost wood that, according to Ernie, has many possibilities for a composition.

and it doesn't do anything for you. Redesign it to be aware suddenly of someone or something," a magic moment, he might have said. "Or have its head twisted around looking at a bug on a twig. That gives it some interest. Or better yet, design it so your eye hits the bird's eye first, then follows the beak and goes out to the bug on the branch, which brings you down to the base and up again. That creates a flow, doesn't it?"

Ernie recalls something that had been bothering him. The World Championship Wildfowl Carving Competition has ruled that compositions for its decorative lifesize pieces, Ernie's owl being one of them, should be designed to be seen from any angle. This was perhaps to keep wall-mounted birds on plaques from being entered. "How do you design a piece that looks good all the way around?" he asks. "The owl

looked good from the front. How could I have made it look good from the back?"

Back to the three chickadees. "Their branch is made of wood left over from the flower business," Ernie says, wrapping his fingers around the walnut base. The wood, called ghost wood, is found in Napa Valley, California. Its twisting branches made their way across the country to be used in flower arrangements, for displaying jewelry, and to hold birds.

"I hold up each piece and twist it and look at it. Sometimes a piece turns you on; some pieces are ugly, rakish-looking, going off in all different directions. Some of the pieces are pretty good, but you can take one that's not and soup it up a little bit or enhance the design by how you work the birds into it." Souping up means adding or removing pieces of branches.

"I have a whole bunch on the lower floor of this

Another piece of ghost wood, a species that can be found in Arizona and California.

building. You spend hours looking through this stuff trying to visualize the driftwood, the base, the birds. I started off with that and designed the chickadees to fit the branches. For these little guys, I started off with one branch and added another one, one that curled around. At first it looked too massive for two birds, so I used three." He remembers that the branch looked good before the chickadees were added. "But I guess the birds actually enhanced the whole thing."

He says the chickadees are looking out at a point about eight inches away where their mother, which never appears, is coming into the composition. The birds are well balanced in terms of posture and arrangement. "A quarter of an inch back or forward and a bird would look wrong," Ernie says. He sees another problem at competitions. "If I see a bird leaning one way or the other, it bothers me. Obviously it didn't

bother the guy putting it together. You hate to see something that's going to fall, but doesn't. I talked about a flying bird, didn't I?" He had. "That, too, leaves you with an uneasy feeling."

But an open space, he says, does not bother him, if it acts as a transitional area. "An empty space is a stopping-off place for the eye after the heads of the birds or the branches carry you along. Take a single shorebird and a shell. You could use the space between them as a third component if it's in the right location." He says there is empty space above the chickadees and below them. But there is still a tight circular area around them, projected by the twisty branches of the ghost wood.

"Some guys, if they live to be three hundred, will never learn good design," he says sharply, picking up the paint brush and removing one of the chickadees from its branch. "Why are some people better at design than others? It's the same with color. Some have good taste in color. They can tell what's pleasing. Aren't women better at color than men?" His reference is to the fact that a significant percentage of men are born with some color limitation.

"I have a good sense of proportion. I don't know, maybe there's an instinct involved with design. I try to balance everything in terms of numbers of birds, placement, color. On the great horned owl, there was so much burnt sienna on the chest that it needed something to counterbalance that color mass. So I used the green of the rhododendron to pull it all together."

He brings his thoughts together and says, "Composition is very essential. I would see it as one of the most important parts of a piece. That's why it would be very helpful to guys to get a good book on flower arranging."

Since the seventh century A.D., flower arranging has been an art form in Japan with a strong and essential component of symbolism. Like most art, the simple flourished and became complex. Massive and elaborate styles developed. A single Japanese flower arrangement might include no fewer than nine visual elements: truth, the highest branch, is accompanied by supporting, receiving, perfectly true, flowing, anterior, body, waiting, and overhanging branches. But the three main branches are truth, supporting, and flowing. These form a triangle with unequal sides. Today, all styles are based on the asymmetrical placement of three principal branches of unequal length to create a Japanese flower composition.

Ernie presents what he has learned about Japanese flower arrangements. "Ikebana," he says, "is the traditional way of arranging flowers in a pattern that's traditionally good. It has been proven to be interesting and good for a thousand years." He describes what he sees in typical Japanese floral arrangements. "They have these three different focal points. The one up high is the main centerline, which is a little off to the right. They call that the heaven part of it. As you come down halfway and to the left of the centerline, you have another mass of flowers or something of interest. That's what they call man. Then down and to the right of the centerline, almost as low as you can get, nearly touching the table, is the earth part.

"When I was making flower arrangements, I started with my center, went to the left, then went to the right as I worked the flowers together. I tried some the other way, say with that man part on the right. But it just didn't look good as the traditional way. Is the brain set up for that?" he wonders aloud.

"A line, a balance of color are things that can help you with your birds. Did somebody else say it or did I say it when I did an interview and mentioned that 'birds are flowers that fly.'" Elaborating on the metaphor, he says, "Birds are colorful. They're like little flowers. They lend themselves well to an arrangement along with some habitat. It's so similar to arranging flowers," he says. "But guys will pay no attention to that. They'll plop a bird in any old position. They don't develop lines so that the piece is interesting, not annoying to the eye." He presents an example. "If you had something sweeping off the base, grass maybe, people would have a hard time concentrating on the bird. The eye would have a tendency to zoom away. But if you had the grasses sweeping toward the bird, you'd develop that circular pattern I was talking about. You would keep the eye entertained."

He reflects for a few moments, adding more wash to the tail of one of the chickadees. He wants to talk more about focal points. He describes a bird's head as a focal point, one that should be pleasing to the viewer. "If you can get a good head, especially a good eye, which is 50 percent of the head, and the head is 50 percent of the body," he says, meaning effort put out by the carver, "you've got it made. You also want good-looking eyes the right size, with pleasant-looking eyelids, and eyes that fit right, not ones bulging out or sunken in or not at the correct angles or too far apart. You can't have a great tail and a lousy head.

"I worked on these chickadees, all my birds, from

The tall piece of wood complements the shape of this long-tailed tit. In the collection of Andy and Sandy Andrews.

The grasses help develop the circular composition of bobwhite quail and fall leaves.

The manzanita wood helps develop a circular flow that is pleasing to look at.

A woodcock with a piece of ghost wood and leaves. The habitat helps develop the design of the piece, encouraging the eye to observe different parts of the composition without leaving it.

The grasses suggest a blowing wind against these semipalmated plovers.

the head out onto the shoulders, to the wings and tail. It seems once you get the heads and eyes where they belong, you can visualize the rest of the bird. If you do the head last, you never get a good piece. If I can look at that little face, it just turns me on. I get more excited to do the rest of the bird. You can relate to it more, get a better feeling for what you're doing. But you still can't let the rest of the piece go to hell because you have a great head on the bird."

He repeats the importance of design while picking up a paper pad and a pencil. He sketches abstractly, making a wispy overlapping centerline and a mass of curly lines at its base. "Sometimes you can take a pencil and paper and just scribble a line on it to develop something." He arches his brows slightly. "This is the quail piece, isn't it? Look, I can put the quail down here," he says, making small egg shapes around the curly mass. He believes the design of his five quail in a desert setting, the piece he titled *Needles, Feathers, and*

Bone, followed the three elements common to the Ikebana done today. He describes the piece in terms of its flow. The main part is the carved cow's skull. He calls it the focal point. "It was the largest mass of color, or absence of color. That's the first place your eye would look. Then your eye would go up to the top of it." That would be the long branch of ghost wood nearly three feet high. He calls it the heaven component. There are several prickly pear cactus leaves, but two of them project at a diagonal above and to the left of the skull. "Your eye should have a tendency to go over that way. Then maybe your eye would look at the birds, then come through the skull to the little cactus sticking out just to the right of the skull. That would be the earth part.

"But none of this is new. It's been studied for a thousand years, and those same lines will still be good a thousand years from now: the centerline or heaven, man on the left, earth on the right."

He relaxes, leaning back in the stool as he applies the wash. "It's interesting, isn't it, these principles. But they aren't etched in stone. You can change them a little bit. They're just a guide, and you can change your piece as to where you want to go with it. Expressions and originality can modify them."

But he complains that judges at competitions often fail to judge design. "They look for details, like counting the number of feathers to see if that's right, or how the color is. They don't judge on the artistic end as much as they should. It's wrong. You have to look at the whole, overall piece, even if the bird is not the right color, or doesn't have the right number of feathers." He shakes his head slightly. "So some guys figure, what's the use of trying to design something super?"

Needles, Feathers, and Bone

The first bird carving competition took place in Bellport, New York, a small town on Long Island's South Shore. This, according to a newspaper account, was a "novel decoy exhibit." The article described the birds as "a delight to the eye," and said that if "men brag some about the superiority of their dummy ducks it would be well to have a competition."

That first bird carvers' convention was held in 1923, nearly three hundred years after the earliest settlers might have combined mud and feathers and a slab of wood to fool the waterfowl they desperately needed for food. When the Bellport competition-exhibition was again held, forty years had passed and it had received a title, the National Decoy Contest. Today, as if National were not inclusive enough, it is called the U.S. National Decoy Contest.

Long Island carvers were not the only ones banding together to test the superiority of their birds. Another competition was formed for Iowans. This one is known as the International Decoy Contest.

In the spirit of competing with the competitions, still more carvers "committeed" and organized what was called in 1968 the Atlantic Flyway Waterfowl &

Bird Carving Exhibit, first held in Salisbury, Maryland. But more important than the starting of another exhibition, a foundation was established that same year. The charter of the Ward Foundation reads in part that a memorial would be created to the Ward Brothers of Crisfield, Maryland; that wildlife art, carvings, antiques, and hunting paraphernalia would be perpetuated and promoted; and that halls, exhibits, and museums would be erected, established, and equipped that would preserve those aspects of wildlife art and hunting.

The Ward Foundation is a memorial to Steve and Lem Ward, both deceased, who made more than "dummy ducks." They put a small piece of art out in the marshes and bays, and today a single bird might be sold for $20,000 or more at an auction.

The exhibits promised in 1968 became an annual competition held now in Ocean City, Maryland. That contest is called the World Championship Wildfowl Carving Competition. The title may convey pretentiousness, but it is not without accuracy and certainly outdoes the national and the international contests. Between ten and twenty thousand visitors are attracted to the Ocean City Convention Center to see birds of all families and species perch, roost, float, fly, and prey on other birds. Eight hundred carvers bring their work, most consciously and agonizingly hoping for a ribbon, blue being preferable to any other color.

There are ribbons for ducks of all species, but, just as important, there are prizes for songbirds, shorebirds, game birds, birds of prey, and seabirds. For three carvers, there is a special award. It is Best in World for a meticulously detailed bird or birds, for a pair of floating ducks that have to be so lifelike that a double take is in order, and for a wildfowl carving in miniature.

Until 1980, the Decorative Lifesize Wildfowl Carving Class put pelicans and turkeys and falcons overshadowing songbirds on the same table and required that the judges pick out the best carving in the

Ernie's first Best-in-World composition was a pair of miniature woodcocks done for the 1979 World Championship Wildfowl Carving Competition. In the collection of the North American Wildlife Art Museum, Salisbury, Maryland.

world—for that year. The complaints were obvious. Was it so easy to discern an apple from an orange when so many differently carved birds were unnaturally flocked together? How could a songbird, no matter how finely tooled, burned, painted, and posed, win over an eagle, even if its feathers were not so well groomed?

Since 1982, families of birds have been designated for the lifesize decorative category. In that year, it was waterfowl, and Canadian Pat Godin won with a pair of black ducks. In 1983 it was shorebirds. A pair of black-crowned night herons took the purchase prize of $18,000. In 1984, the designated family was game birds. A group of five bobwhite quail in a desert setting won. It was done by Ernie Muehlmatt. And in 1985, it was birds of prey. Ernie's great horned owl did not win.

Winning Best in World in those three areas means substantial prize money. In 1985, it was $20,000 for the lifesize decorative carving, $10,000 for the floating waterfowl, and $7,500 for the miniature. It also means that the bird or birds are placed in a small museum on the campus of a small college in Salisbury, Maryland. The downstairs part of the museum might have been administrative offices before the changeover. Now glass cubes rest on bases. Inside them are Best-in-World pieces along with compositions from the years when birds were on the wing, usually in some stop-action pursuit of another bird. In one large glass case, a peregrine falcon attacks a flock of green-winged teal among fall cornstalks. In another, a hawk has forever clutched the feather of a pheasant in one set of talons. The pheasant itself has yet to be caught and killed.

Ernie does not discount his two Best-in-World

The woodcocks are half-size.

Another closeup of what Ernie describes as a simple piece with woodcocks nestled in leaves and wood.

miniature titles, but he is not loquacious about them either. In 1979, he went to the competition with a pair of half-size woodcocks in a setting of rocks and fallen leaves. Between and behind the birds is a spiny branch with a single leaf that is on the verge of falling. Two years later he returned with a pair of least bitterns, characteristically camouflaging themselves in tall grasses. He won the miniature title again.

Predictably, he says that winning the Best-in-World title in 1984 was that one great moment of his life, the moment most people would compare to a honeymoon, a first healthy child, winning a sizeable lottery.

Shortening this World Championship simply to the World, as most carvers do, Ernie says, "Last year at the World, I was disappointed to win third place with my owl. But I guess it's better than being in fourth place.

A closeup of the bitterns and grasses. The dark colors were burned on the birds.

Ernie's second Best-in-World piece was these least bitterns, done for the 1981 World Championship. Ernie says the birds are similar but curved in different directions. In the collection of the North American Wildlife Art Museum, Salisbury, Maryland.

Skunk cabbage makes up part of the habitat. This is the way it looks when it first comes out of the ground.

They announce third place first, you know. But at least you're in the top three. Well, that's the way it goes."

Ernie recounts how he had three woodcocks in the competition when in 1983 the theme, as the Ward

This composition, entitled Needles, Feathers, and Bone, *won* Best in World *for the Decorative Lifesize Wildfowl Carving category in 1984. In the collection of the North American Wildfowl Art Museum, Salisbury, Maryland. Photo courtesy of the Ward Foundation.*

Foundation describes it, was shorebirds. "Woodcocks, although thought of as game birds, can be found along the shore," he explains. "It was a nice piece, and everybody I talked to said I had a good chance of getting somewhere, maybe second or third. So you listen to that all weekend and you think, 'Well, maybe I do have a shot.' So when it came time to announce the winners, the third place was given first. And it wasn't me. I figured I got second place. Then that was announced and it wasn't me again. I said, 'Oh, God, I can't be the first? That would be too much to ask.' But then they announced first place and it wasn't me. It's a letdown and you feel jerked around."

He swishes his brush in his wash of burnt umber, stirring it rapidly. "I entered the decorative lifesize category three or four times. One year I had a screech owl being harassed by two sparrows. That didn't do anything. Another year I had a set of meadowlarks on a fencepost. That came in fourth. And I had the quail entered. And the great horned owl came in third. So I won one out of five times."

In 1986, the theme was seabirds. Ernie had no entry. But in 1987 the theme will be songbirds. "I have no idea what to do. Do you have any good ideas? I thought of doing four and twenty blackbirds baked in a pie. Instead of carving a skull, I'll carve a pie with the birds coming out of it."

He laughs and says, "For this World show, you have to do something worth $20,000. How do you make a bunch of songbirds interesting and worth that much? It would be hard to do just a pair."

The 1984 winner of the Best-in-World title and the runners-up to Ernie's left: Anthony Rudisill and Grant Goltz. On the far left is Sam Dyke, Chairman of the Ward Foundation, and to Ernie's immediate left is Knute Bartrug, Chairman Emeritus of the Ward Foundation. Photo courtesy of the Ward Foundation.

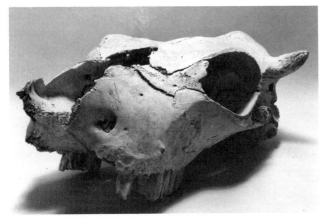

The skull Ernie used as a model for the carved skull of the Needles, Feathers, and Bone *composition.*

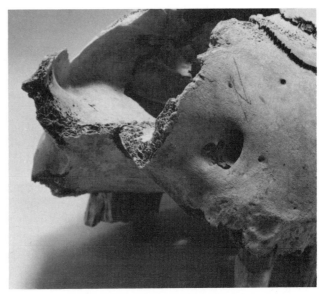

The marrow that had to be duplicated.

He did more than a pair of birds for the composition that won him $20,000 in 1984. He did five birds, one on top of a fleshless and disintegrating cow's skull, with cactus plants and a twisting branch of wood in the background. He called the piece *Needles, Feathers, and Bone.*

He knew he wanted quail. The designated family that year was game birds, and Ernie had already carved a hundred quail, making their brown and black patterns from the thousands of lines scored by a burning tool.

Bobwhite quail are considered the most popular game bird in North America. In the United States, they are primarily found in the eastern and southern states, from North Dakota to Texas. Social birds, they are likely to group together, and a unit (called a covey) may have up to fifteen birds.

"I knew I wanted a group of quail at different heights, and I knew I wanted a desert setting," Ernie says. "Someone questioned whether you can find them in the desert. Well, I checked the books and they said you can find bobwhite quail just about anywhere.

"Anyway," he says, exaggerating the word, "I thought of using a rock to get some height, and I thought of using a chunk of driftwood. But everybody does that, and you don't find much driftwood out in the desert. A lot of succulent plants, but not much in the way of trees."

He points to a skull hanging on a nail on the wall near his Foredom station. It is fleshless, weather-fatigued, and gray. A few of the teeth of this cow's head gone to bone are missing, and cracks run along its length. "I found that skull on Wye Island," he explains. "Oh, I guess twenty years ago my wife and I

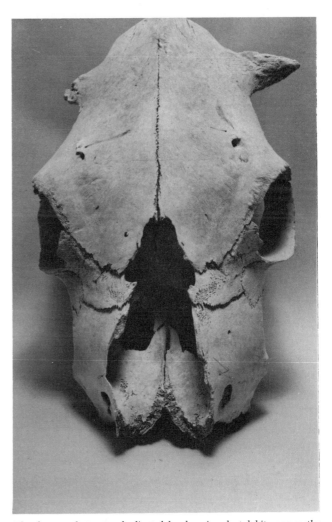

The fissures that were duplicated by dragging dental bits across the wood.

were doing some boating down on the Chester River in Maryland and we pulled up to an island that had cows grazing in a pasture. Evidently, diseased cows were left there for the buzzards to pick away at. There were quite a few cows left like that. And there was this almost mint-condition skull with all the meat picked off it."

The skull was taken home and took up space in his wife's rock garden for five or six years. The cracks, he says, were made by the action of freezing and thawing, which also exposed bits of marrow. For an almost equal amount of time it hung in the room of one of his sons, a boy who himself may have dreamed of desert settings. He later moved west and worked at shoeing horses for a time. Its next destination was the room below his studio, where it hung for another five or six years.

"So what's the point of all this? One day I was downstairs and I saw this cow's skull and I said, 'Hey, I'll have one quail standing up on the skull and the others gathered around it.'" He prolongs a smile.

"Now I had to figure out how I was going to carve wood to look like bone. I started out with tupelo, no, it was jelutong. It doesn't really matter." He sounds annoyed with this gap in his memory. "No, it was jelutong, two pieces that I glued up because I couldn't get a single piece big enough. So how do you make a pattern from a cow's skull?" he asks. "Well, you make a side-view pattern. Not a heck of a big deal, but when I cut it out, it was still a square block of wood. So I took out a big carbide cutter and made tons of sawdust all over the place," he coughs as if by reflex, "and finally got it shaped. I had a little bit of trouble getting the skull hollowed out inside, but a little bit each day and it came around."

The exterior of the skull still had to be textured and painted. "I took some little tiny dental bits and sat there for days cutting fissures and holes and the marrowy parts of the bone, trying to duplicate every little detail I could. For those fissures, I would drag the dental bit up and down the wood. That was neat," he says. But it was not all fun. "I got sick and tired of sitting there putting cracks and fissures in the wood. Finally I decided it was good enough."

He remembers the look of the carved skull, by then more bone than wood. "I almost hated to put an undercoat on it, it looked so good," he says, admitting, though, that he was afraid he would lose the appearance of weathered bone. "But I did. I undercoated with this Krylon 1301 acrylic spray stuff and put a

The carved skull. Photo courtesy of the Ward Foundation.

couple of coats of gesso on it. So far, so good. It still looked bony.

"Then I put on one or two washes of ultramarine blue and burnt umber to gray it up. Then I thought, should I continue on or leave it?" He answered his own question when he saw that it was still too light for aged bone. He looked at the real skull again and saw what appeared to be a mottled effect. It had blotches of gray. "So I took some more washes and a big dry brush. . . ." He stops to reach for it on his paint turntable. Not finding it, he says, "I guess Jeff borrowed it," meaning his son who has returned from the West to shoe horses in the East. "Anyway, I took the brush and the wash, blotted the brush, and dabbed at the skull and got this mottled effect. Then I put my last wash on and, thank God, it worked out." He lets out a small laugh of relief.

Ernie accepted that there is more to a desert than a cow's skull. Cactus has a strong association with deserts, and he chose to re-create cactus plants for the composition. But the cacti would serve another function. Their green would color-complement the browns and burnt siennas of the bobwhite quail, perhaps even make the quail project more when viewed in front of a cactus segment or two.

It was another island that supplied this component. Ernie and his wife had vacationed on Long Beach Island off the coast of New Jersey. There, prickly pear cactus is a native plant. Taking some home for carving models, he also purchased cacti from a local flower shop and made patterns of the segments. These he cut from half-inch-thick jelutong, "rough-carved them with a Foredom, then sanded them with concave bumps and concaves," he says.

Most cactus plants have needles or spines that are

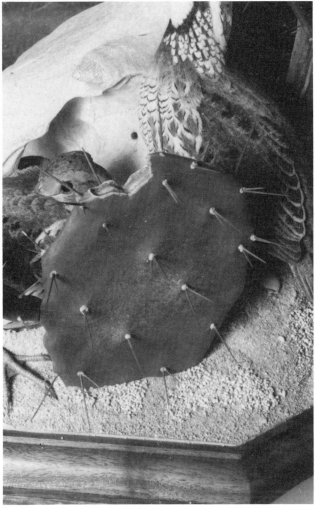

A cactus with a bite out of it. Photo courtesy of the Ward Foundation.

A horned toad hiding in the skull cavity. Photo courtesy of the Ward Foundation.

paired. To duplicate these, he used birch toothpicks and fitted each one into a chuck attached to his stationary motor. Wrapping sandpaper around the turning toothpick created a slender needle. "I remember working all day making cactus needles. I thought I had a mountain of them. The next day I applied them and got through only one cactus. And I had nine or ten cactus leaves all together." He finally made about 450 needles.

One of the cactus segments has a bitelike break at its top. A real cactus would reveal a fleshy inside protected by a harder outer skin. The outer skin of Ernie's consisted of roughly thirty layers of acrylic washes and matte medium to enhance a shiny finish.

"Matte medium is like a thick water," Ernie says of the polymer medium often used as a vehicle for dry pigments or as a thinner for acrylic colors. "It doesn't

have a tendency to bead up. Washes go on nice and smooth on top of that. But it builds up, so I had to blot some of it off. Oh, I guess I put ten coats of it on the cactus plants for a paraffin or waxy look." He digresses. "But I never use it on a wooden bird. It has a tendency to build up on the burns and you lose a lot of detail. Well, I do put it on the bill for a bony look. Other than that, I don't see a use for it," he concludes.

But he was not yet satisfied with the look of the cactus leaves. When he found a bag of extremely fine marble dust in a closet, he made a quick connection. He dusted each segment with the pulverized marble, which suggested desert dust. But don't cactus plants also have a blotchy look? he asked himself, perhaps thinking about the skull as well. He finally and finely sprayed the plants with water in a Windex bottle.

Since those earlier years when habitat displays engulfed a bird with an array of flora and indigenous fauna, carvers struggled with when and where to add design components that would complement a bird, yet not overpower it or detract from it. Ernie wanted a horned toad as part of his desert, already inhabited by birds, plants, and a cow long dead. He located a taxidermied toad, carved it, then wondered where to place it. It now peaks out of the left eye socket of the skull, slightly hidden by paper grasses growing in the same cavity. His justification was simple. A toad would not want to be conspicuous, even if bobwhite quail are basically vegetarians.

There is more to the composition than the intrinsic sense of place—a desolate locale, yet capable of supporting life. The quail themselves tell a story. On the right side there is a hen quail with her head turned around in a resting position. He describes this as the

Two of the five bobwhite quail of the composition. The lower bird is a hen, the upper a male. Photo courtesy of the Ward Foundation.

most interesting bird. "She has one leg stretched out," Ernie explains, "and you can feel the kinetics, the tension of that bird trying to keep from sliding off that sandy slope she's on. She's trying to keep her balance." The bird immediately to the hen's left is alert. "It's the one peeking over the top of the skull. What's the commotion that's disturbing the other ones?" he asks for the bird. "But the bird on the side of the bank hasn't noticed you yet. She's more interested in not sliding off the hill than in looking at you." He nods slightly to himself, as if approving of what he had done. "Yeah, I guess this is a magic moment. It's that moment of contact before the birds decide they'd better take off."

The center bird is perched on the top of the skull, its head beginning to come around for greater eye contact. The one to the left of that one stands on a projecting branch. And the one next to it is on the sandy knoll or drift under the skull, its body facing away from the observer, its head turned 90 degrees to its right.

The branch the one quail stands on is a piece of manzanita tree, one of many relics of Ernie's floral design days now finding places as branches for carved birds to rest on.

"Like I said before, I needed something to give height to some quail in a desert theme. You don't find driftwood in a desert, you find flat ground. So what else would you use for a bird to stand on out in the desert? So I have one bird standing on a little piece of manzanita about three inches up. Then another bird is on top of the cow skull. Next to it is a bird on the ground." Pausing, organizing his thoughts, he continues, "That's working from left to right. So I had three different heights. There's a flow." He laughs and says, "There's those circles again. They bring your eye around and around.

"Another carver said I could have done without that stick. But I thought it would add something to it, like frosting on a cake. It didn't hinder it. It kept the eye in the piece. I think it was pretty strong on design. It had heaven, earth, and man, didn't it?"

One of his comments on design prompts him to bring back to the painting station a book he had been reading. The soft-cover book is devoted to the art of Raymond Ching. About ten years younger than Ernie and New Zealand-born, Ching is a painter whose works exhibit a dramatic realism, almost a photorealism that at times puts a bird and its surroundings on a white background.

Ernie reads aloud portions of the author's commentary on Ching and his paintings. "Look here," he says, "he talks about how tempting it is to compromise. And here he says just the act of painting is going to create problems." He looks up from the book. "With that owl, there were endless problems on how to get the feet at the right levels, and how to fasten the wings to the body, and how to drape the dead quail over the stump to make it look dead, and how to re-create the texture of the dead cow skull, and how to get the juicy look to the cactus. Did you ever think of how we use the same mediums of paint and wood and get all this different stuff with them? You're dealing with the softness of feathers; the hard, bony texture of a skull; the pulpy juiciness of the cactus."

He returns to the book. "This guy writes that solving problems is part of a creative process and it drains the artist and he becomes depressed." He recalls the months of February and March in 1985, months spent on a great horned owl, the composition of which would be finished only two days before he had to go to Ocean City with it. "The more I worked on that owl, the more depressed and anxious I got. And then when you finish a piece, according to Ching, you can't stand looking at it anymore.

"That cow skull I worked on for weeks. Days and days I sat there with my Foredom and a needle-sharp carbide cutter cutting fissures in what was to look like a dried, cracked surface," he says. His precise imagery presented how difficult the process really was. "And where parts were chipped off you could see the marrowy honeycomb pock marks. I sat there for days putting those in. I could have gone for another week, but I just wanted to get it out of my sight."

He leans back on the stool. He picks out one more sentence from the book and tries to rephrase it. "Agony. That's what Ching talks about. The best works of art don't tell anybody about the agony the artist went through. And nobody knows how I suffered with that owl and that skull."

Pebbles, Patterns, and Polyurethane Birds

"Habitat is not my favorite thing," Ernie states as he rotates a brush in a jar of opaque water. "But sometimes you have to do it for a good composition." His formulas for habitat displays are simple. "Leaves, grass, some flowers can be done with paper. When I make a paper leaf, I trace around a real leaf and make a paper pattern, cut the leaves out of shopping bags or brown craft paper, paint them with a mixture of water and acrylic paints, then let them dry. After they're dry so the acrylics won't run, I wet the leaf slightly and, with a dull burning pen on a padding or towel or anything soft, I burn the veins in, or the stems, or bug marks, or holes, or whatever I see." He pauses, then continues. "Usually by the time I'm done burning, they're dry again and nicely shaped." Burning on one side of a paper leaf causes it to curl upward. "You can get S-curves or compound curves—interesting curvatures."

He says the best material, one used by most other carvers interested in replicating stones and pebbles, is a powder called Durham's Rock Hard Water Putty. "On the *Needles, Feathers, and Bone* piece," Ernie says, "I needed to make a whole bunch of different pieces of

sand and gravel, and I didn't want to use real sand and gravel." World competition judges feel the use of natural materials such as real stones or a real cow's skull detract from the originality of the composition.

What helps facilitate stone- and gravel-making is what Ernie describes as "a little hand-operated cement mixer, nothing more than two plastic bowls that you put together with the putty inside." He compares it to a cocktail mixer. "You mix the putty according to the directions into a claylike ball about the size of a golf ball. Then you chop it up with a putty knife into marble-size chunks, sprinkle them with a little dry putty while the pieces are still in the maleable state, put the two bowls together, and shake them vigorously for two or three minutes."

The result is a number of marble-size balls, some of which can be saved for stones of that size. The rest can be divided into pea-size pieces and sprinkled with dry putty. Again, the two bowls mix the material, and round, pea-size balls result. The next step, Ernie says, is to make BB-size pieces. Repeating the process once more, sand-size pieces can be made. Finally, "You lay out whatever you have on a piece of newspaper until

A beech leaf made out of a paper grocery bag. The distresses and bug holes were put in with a burning pen.

A paper oak leaf that can be incorporated into a habitat display.

it all dries. That takes about an hour. Then, with different-size sieves, you sort them out into sand size, pea size, BB size. If you want some of the pieces cracked, just hit them with a hammer."

He explains how to apply putty, sand, and gravel to a base. He uses a material sold by most suppliers of bird-carving tools called Tuf Carv. Available as a polyester resin with a separate hardening agent, the material is described in catalogs as a light-colored wood filler that can be sawed, milled, sanded, and ground with rotary tools. Once it is set in a recessed wooden base, he applies matte medium over it before it is hard and puts the artificial stones and gravel over that. "Leave it sit until it's dry, turn it over, and dump the excess off." He says most of the Durham putty pebbles will stick. "If you want more on, rewet it with matte medium, add more stones and gravel, let that dry, and keep working at it."

Durham's Rock Hard Water Putty made these various-sized stones and pebbles.

Ernie can also make an earthy composition with Durham's Rock Hard Water Putty or with automobile body putty. Either filler can be worked by poking at it with a brush. If he were working paint this way, the process would be called stippling. Usually he will pour the filler on wax paper set inside a recessed base. Doing this prevents the putty from sticking to the wood. It can then be lifted out, shaped, reshaped, and set back in without risking damage to the surrounding base.

He explains that either filler starts to set up in minutes, though that time can be adjusted by the amount of hardener used. "I jab at it with a stiff brush while it's still in the loose stage and distress the surface to get the look of soil. Then I coat that with matte medium and paint it with acrylics to get the colors I want: dirt, moss, even snow." A spruce grouse he had carved was

Preparing a base for a meadowlark. Ernie will use automobile body putty or a wood filler called Tuf Carv.

He first draws the exact size of the base on a piece of paper, which in turn will be covered with wax paper.

Mixing the body putty with its hardener.

The mix of the previous step is poured onto the pattern. This gives a rough size. Then the bird and its base are placed in position and the mix is allowed to harden around the wood. But before it has hardened, it can be shaped to simulate earth. The wax paper allows the body putty base to be removed. It is then cut with a saw to fit the octagon base, which was purchased from Birds of a Feather. (See appendix for address.)

composed with a winter setting. He explains, "It looked like snow. I coated it with matte medium, then sprinkled the filler with very fine valspar stone on top of that and painted that white. It looked for all the world like snow."

He moves the chickadees, their branch, and their base in front of him. "Habitat is something we have to think about. We have to put design into the birds themselves, not their bases. You've got to use less and less stuff. If I put leaves and grasses with these birds, they wouldn't add a thing to the piece; it would just give your eye another place to go jumping around to. It would destroy the piece."

The three chickadees that have had several thin washes of grays and browns to lighten and darken areas stand warmed by the air generated by the hairdryer. Ernie lets the brush hover over his mixing tray and points finally toward his bandsaw station. "I make a lot of false starts," he says. He also calls them duds. "On the workbench, there are two duds for these baby chickadees. There's a whole box of duds over there from *Needles, Feathers, and Bone.* I did twelve quail to get the five I wanted. And the owl took three bodies to get one."

He believes, then, that the painting, not the carving, is the easiest process in creating birds. "When I'm painting, I can talk to someone else. It doesn't bother me. But when I'm shaping the bird, it takes a lot of intense thought. I need to concentrate. I guess it's because I'm not dead sure of where I'm going. If I were, nothing would bother me." He replaces a deep frown with a grin.

"I guess the carving is the weakest part of what I do," he says, shrugging his shoulders slightly. "Burning is fairly easy, painting is easy, but getting the initial shape, getting out of wood what I want the bird to be, is hard. So many things can go wrong. But you can't very well mess up a paint job the way I paint with these washes." He reexplains the thinness of the acrylic wash, the cellophane quality that tones down or enhances a previous coat. "With burning, you can sand it out and start all over again" (which he does not do). "But with carving, if you take too much out in one spot, you're licked. You start all over again. That's what made me nervous with that owl. But once that was over and I got to sanding it, it was duck soup. And the painting I got done in a couple of days."

He has a theory for initial shaping that begins with a paramilitary expression. "The main thing is to just blast in there and not be afraid to make mistakes. But get started and do something, whether it's right or wrong. If it's bad, you get another chunk of wood. But in the first half hour, you can tell whether you're on the right track. If the bird doesn't look absolutely perfect, you have to throw it away. You can't correct it by overworking it.

"I think the faster you get it out of the wood, rough-shaped, the better you are. Use your fastest cutter, your fastest machine." Ernie will use a bandsaw for most of the rough shaping. He first compares the process to doing a rough sketch. Then he alludes to his art school training. "We'd have a model in front of us and she'd strike a pose for two or three seconds, and you'd have to capture that in a short time, four or five seconds—just get the essence of what she was doing in four or five seconds.

"John Scheeler says the same thing about getting it roughed out." The reference is to a friend, a carver with three dozen best-in-show awards and seven World Championships from the World Competition. His specialty, capturing the wild look, has been birds of prey. Great horned owls, goshawks, prairie falcons, and other raptors have taken shape in his home in Mays Landing, New Jersey. "He says the quicker you get it out of the wood, get your sketch onto the wood and get it shaped the way you want it, the better it is. If you sit and mess around with it and take a little bit off here and there, you're sunk. You've got to go at it like the end of the world was coming this afternoon. If you're afraid to take wood away, you get bogged down in details and never get anywhere."

He reflects for a moment, rotating the paint brush between thumb and forefinger. "I guess this would be good if you were out in the field doing sketches.

"Anyway," he prolongs the word, "in fifteen minutes you should know if you're on the right track. Then you get slower and slower until you're down to the fine tuning." He refers to detailing the body with characteristic feather bumps, muscles, and facial features. He nods approvingly. "I would say that's what I would do. Now if I could only see color." He lets out an abrupt, ironic laugh.

"I guess this relates to why I don't like to use patterns." He makes a gesture toward a two-drawer, army-green filing cabinet. In it are correspondence, photographs, and file folders of patterns.

Despite what he says, he has hundreds of patterns in that cabinet. For a chickadee, there are close to two dozen. He attempts to explain why he files patterns, nearly all of which were used only once. "In the begin-

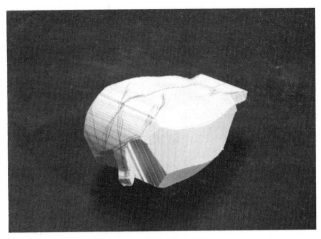

A bandsawed chickadee removed from its block with as few cuts as possible. This can be done in less than a minute.

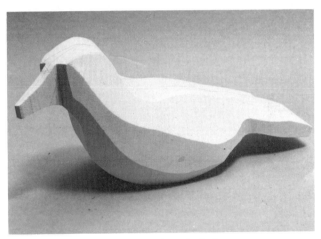

A bandsawed meadowlark.

Fifteen minutes after the bandsawing, this roughed-out meadowlark can be achieved.

ning I had trouble coming up with good patterns, but once you know the anatomy of the bird, its lumps and bumps, well, it's not hard," he says easily.

He explains what he believes to be a generic anatomical description of a bird. The body, he says, is egg-shaped. "You put another little bump on the front for the chest, another circle for the head, lengthen or narrow it so it can assume the personality of the bird you want to do, and thicken or thin the tail. Then work on the bill.

"For most birds, whether a goose or one of these chickadees, you start out with that egg shape. With the tail, you can have it up or down. A woodcock has a stumpy tail; a cardinal has an elongated tail. But the body of a bird doesn't change." Unlike a mammal such as a human, a bird does not have a flexible spinal cord. "No matter how the body twists, the only parts movable are the head and neck," though he adds that the rump or rear can move up, down, or sideways, which makes the tail move correspondingly.

Ernie taught a seminar for an audience of several hundred people and brought along a Foredom, study skins, a slide viewer, and a manikin. "I made up a movable manikin of a quail," he says, one made of cardboard and paper rivets. "I had an egg for the body and a movable chunk for the rump, held together with a little bolt so it could move up and down. I did the same for the neck. That moved. With all that, I could make a sleeping bird, an alert bird, a feeding bird. I could put that manikin into any position and get fifty different quail patterns. It was a very valuable gadget."

Still, he is reluctant to rely on patterns, counterpointing what he just explained. "Paper manikins are good for people who don't know how to draw. If I were doing a quail right now, or another set of chickadees, I'd get a mental picture of them rather than going to the files and dragging out a pattern. I guess I understand what the problem is with carvers. They have trouble drawing." His tone gets serious. "But you should learn to draw. Get a good photo if you can, one of a side view, but don't copy someone else's and don't take a pattern from a painting," he says dogmatically. He gestures toward a framed print of a meadowlark hanging near his Foredom station. "You could put a piece of tracing paper over that. It's life-size. You'd get a dandy pattern. But it wouldn't be *your* pattern."

He muses for a moment. "Maybe the guy who can't draw had better take some drawing lessons or classes." People say to him that he was born with a talent to make artistic lines or outlines on paper. He disagrees.

"Maybe you're born with a tendency to draw, but you still have to learn to draw. I've been drawing since I was two years old. Just the shear amount of drawing taught me." He remembers that his first drawings were terrible.

He continues his criticism of patterns. "When you copy someone else's pattern, it's not your bird." He points out that prolific carvers who do fine birds have stylistic trademarks. Owing to a pose, usually, or an expressive face, their birds become recognizable. He says his carver friend Jim Sprankle's waterfowl are easily identifiable. "You can always tell a Sprankle bird, can't you?" Ernie says. "What is it? Benign interest in the world?"

He is also critical of study skins and mounted birds. Though there are federal laws protecting songbirds, many dead ones, vaguely described as road kills, find their way to museums and nature centers. There they are available for study by artists and carvers who carry sketch pads and calipers. But the process of death immediately affects the quality of the remains, regardless of how quickly taxidermy work is done. The beak or bill of a bird, being as much flesh as bone, begins to shrink. Its color fades as does the color of the legs and feet, and the feathers, if not kept out of direct sunlight, will also lose their colors to fading.

Ernie prefers to take only a few measurements from stuffed or mounted birds. An overall length and the distance between the eye channels are two measurements he uses. But his basic approach is, he says, to use his eyes. "You've got to get a feel for the bird when you're shaping. You've got to eyeball it. Engineers are crazy about measurements," he says, a direct reference to students he has had. "They carry slide rules. They're building a bird, not carving one. It's not the way to do it." His way is to sculpt it quickly with the bandsaw and turn the flat planes left by the saw into rounded-off wood with sanding and grinding tools.

Several carvers are marking cast birds to be used as references. Ernie too makes birds cast in resin, but refuses to sell them to be copied. As it is, he says, "You can spot a Muehlmatt bird a mile away when somebody's copied one. And I wouldn't want somebody painting up one of these castings himself and calling that a Muehlmatt bird."

Made of a liquid polyurethane, Ernie's cast birds have been made from carved pieces, which in turn were molded in rubber. The pourings he does himself on his painting table, diagonally opposite to where he applies washes. One of his castings shows birds com-

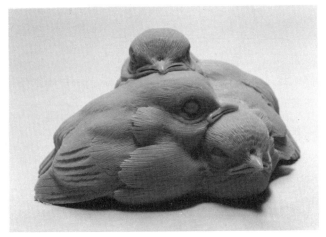

A casting of baby chickadees Ernie titled First Night Out.

A look down into the silicon rubber mold Ernie uses to make his polyurethane cast birds. Reversing the photo shows an almost three-dimensional view of the impression.

pactly clustered together, a small sphere of three baby chickadees. Another is of two immature wrens. These he sells for $150 a casting after he has painted them. He compares what he does to the canvas artist who sells prints.

He reveals there is little work involved. "With a little bit of painting, one of these can be sold for one-tenth the cost of an original." He has brought an unpainted chickadee cluster to his paint table. There are nine others on a box table below his rear window. "I'll sell ten to fifteen of them at a show, and it's good pocket money," he admits. "I made the original for this one out of a piece of jelutong. You just buy silicon rubber, pour that over the original, let it harden, break it free, get the original out of the rubber, and use that as your mold. Using a two-part polyurethane mixed together makes the birds." He says it will harden in five minutes, though it has to be left alone for half an hour. Cracks might occur if it's taken prematurely out of the mold, which is peeled away. A rubber mold, he says, is good for fifty pieces before it starts to break. "With a little bit of cleaning up, I can take some of the flares off. Just excess plastic. Then I'm ready to paint. I undercoat each casting with matte medium because plastic has a tendency to repel water. It makes a nice surface.

"These are a lot more fun to paint than a wooden bird," he says. "With a wooden bird, you have to get the paint to flow properly. But I still wouldn't sell them unpainted. I'd hate to see a lousy paint job on one of these in someone's house and hear someone say that it's a Muehlmatt bird when it isn't."

A pair of cast baby Carolina wrens.

The painted casting of Carolina wrens.

The wooden original model for the baby wrens.

The rear of the casting.

This is a casting of a group of chickadees carved in the shape of an Easter egg that was displayed at the White House. Ernie was one of some thirty artists chosen to paint eggs for an Easter Sunday presentation. Unhappy with his painted egg, he decided to carve one. He calls this piece Chickadee Dumpty.

He finds something else that will channel his thoughts back to his great horned owl project. He remembers having to interrupt work on the bird, though he doesn't recall at what stage. Perhaps it was when the dead quail was carved, and the owl had yet to be found in the wood. Or it may have been when it lacked its 15 miles of burning lines, or when he decided to make the head and body as one piece. "I was running out of money, so I had to do some molded birds. But while I was working on those, I was worried about getting the owl done. It was hard to go three months without any money, with bills to pay and a kid in college. Most carvers live from day to day anyway. We don't put any money away," he says, modulating his voice.

He has done three or four hundred molded clusters of birds, he estimates. He can paint ten of these sets in a day, given a long day, and has no trouble finding buyers. One of the groupings, called *First Night Out*, sells for $150. At a show, he sells between ten and fifteen castings.

Though he finds the painting fun, he admits that going through so many at a time bores him. "It's more exciting doing a bird with some meat on it," he says, "where you don't know exactly what you're doing, something where you figure it all out as you're going along. Sometimes stuff that's too easy is not very rewarding." The owl again returns to the conversation. "The hardest thing I ever did was that owl. And the most rewarding thing I ever did was that owl."

He says it was sold to a collector and patron of bird carvers, H. P. "Andy" Andrews. The president of a camshaft plant in Jackson, Michigan, Andrews buys from Ernie and other carvers. Some of the pieces

The painted casting.

go into a museumlike setting in his home, the rest are resold at Wild Wings Decoy Den, a gallery in Tampa, Florida. Ernie wears a sweater with the gallery insignia.

The owl, which was bought in Ocean City immediately after the judging for the 1985 Wildfowl Carving Competition, was not Andrews' only purchase from Ernie. "I would say Andy has bought between fifty and a hundred pieces. I think he probably buys more carvings and artwork in the wildlife end of it than anybody else in the United States," he adds with certainty.

He will do commissioned pieces such as quail and woodcocks for the gallery, and he does baby chickadees on pieces of ghost wood. "If I didn't want to do things for Andy, I guess I would customize my works for another kind of customer. Probably little birds like single chickadees. I guess I would do more shows. I would have more castings, things to appeal to the small collector. Big pieces are hard to sell," he explains, "but in a gallery they eventually go," though he adds with a laugh that a grouping of great blue herons, birds which average four feet in height, would not easily leave even a gallery.

He says his chickadees, the wooden mature kind, sell for $600. Sparrows go for $100 more than that. More detail justifies the difference, he says. Woodcocks are tough to do, he says, with complicated feather patterns and miles of burning lines. This game bird will sell for nearly ten times the price of a chickadee. And a grouse like the spruce grouse he did was sold for approximately twenty times the price of the chickadee.

"If you spend a tremendous amount of time on a bird that no one knows, you probably couldn't give it away. But chickadees are simple birds. They're popular; they don't take much time. People will buy them." But he wonders whether they sell for more than they are worth.

"It's very difficult pricing your things. A lot of guys who start carving have that problem. And you can go up, but you can never, ever come down." He elaborates on his economic theory. "If you start with a $600 chickadee or higher, for the rest of your life you have to stay with a $600 chickadee. In my case, where I've sold thousands of chickadees, if someone goes to a show and sees one of my birds for $300, he's going to wonder what happened and isn't going to buy any more birds. It's very easy to get on a roll and think you're hot stuff and raise your prices, but you can get to a point where you wish you hadn't." It happened to

One of Ernie's acrylic paintings that was made into prints. This one of a woodcock was based on a carving.

Another print of a bobwhite quail.

A painted wooden golden eagle head set on a piece of marble to represent a mountain habitat.

This is the original painting of a pair of ruffed grouse.

This eagle was borrowed form a college restaurant. The head was used as a model for carvings and castings.

him, he admits. "I overpriced myself, but fortunately my career moved ahead, so my birds were worth that new price."

Winning a World Championship moves a career ahead, he says, which is what happened to him. He stares at his chickadees and says, "This pricing business is tough."

Not everything has been chickadees, woodcocks, and cast birds. He did try three watercolors, two of which ended up lithographed. Hundreds remain under a countertop between his burning and his painting stations. The two he brings to shows are vignettes, images of birds and their habitats in the centers of otherwise white paper. One is a woodcock with a heaven-bound branch behind it, the other a bobwhite quail on a piece of branching wood with fall oak leaves at its feet. The third is still unprinted and unhung in his studio. Two ruffed grouse rest in green leaves. All three look like Muehlmatt carvings because he used his carved birds and their minimal habitats as models.

Ernie even tried to share his work in the medium of bronze. He calls his effort, simply, "a departure from songbirds and game birds." It started with a television show. He remembers Alexander Haig being interviewed. "I was watching the show, and on Haig's desk for just a split second I thought I saw a bald eagle's head on a block of wood. So I said, 'I'm going to do a bald eagle head on a block of something.'"

The model for the eagle did not come from a museum or as a road kill, but from a college restaurant. "It had about eighty years of cooking grease all over it. It was terrible looking," he says, "but it was good for

A golden eagle head carved in jelutong. Bronze castings were made from it.

The original wood carving for a bald eagle head. Bronze castings were made from this.

what I wanted. It had all the right dimensions, but the color was a complete disaster. I used it as a model. It was a bald eagle. Later I made a golden eagle head, and had them both cast in bronze."

The bronzes were not well received. They did not, as he puts it, "set the world on fire." He says, "I think out in the West people are more attuned to bronzes, but I sold a few. I thought I would mount the golden eagle heads on chunks of marble," a material he thought was part of the eagle's mountain habitat. "I was pleased with them, though. I enjoyed seeing the wax process before the casting, the finishing.

"It was interesting doing the bronzes, watching that process, doing the prints, watching the color separations. It gave me a better understanding of the bronze artist, the flatwork artist. You realize that stuff doesn't just appear at a show or gallery by magic. A lot of hard work was involved."

Pewter Feet and Ruby Carvers

Ever since carvers decided to turn from the flat-bottomed decoy to birds that would stand, perch, or fly, they have had to deal with the problems of making feet. Feet for flying birds are almost decorative in function, but for a standing bird, feet have to be engineered for strength. Depending on the size of the bird, wooden feet, difficult in themselves to sculpt, would not hold the body with any assurance that sagging or total failure would not occur. Other strategies, then, were devised. One has been to make a leg armature out of a strong wire and add toes to that with solder or an epoxy putty. The other has been to buy feet ready-made and cast in pewter, a combination of lead and tin.

Ernie remembers the history of pewter feet. He thinks Jack Holt of Wilmington, Delaware, was one of the first bird carvers to make and use cast feet. "We were down at his house for dinner one night, and he showed me how he made feet with a mold. He used silicon rubber for the mold and used actual birds' feet he got from a nature center. Everyone else was pounding them out of lead at the time. Here, let me show you," he says, reaching behind him for a steel cylinder about two inches high. In it, looking like an archaeological fossil, was an imprint of a small bird's foot. "We would carve the shape of a bird's foot in reverse, then lay a piece of sheet lead over that, pound on it, take a pair of snippers, and trim the excess off. That was the foot.

"Nobody was making them commercially, so being the lazy guy that I am," he says without conviction, "I had a guy who was working for me develop them to sell." He describes a carpenter he had working part-time to convert the highway building into a studio. He was also cutting out bird blanks and helping with classes. "He was very interested in this procedure for making feet, so he went home and experimented with it. Oh, there was another guy from Lansdowne [Pennsylvania] who was playing with pewter feet molds. So I took some titmouse feet to him and he made a mold and cast some for me. But there was too much lead in them, and they sagged. So then I got Rick Delise, that's the carpenter, to make the molds and feet. He put more tin in the lead to stiffen the feet. He started going to bird shows and went at it pretty big. Now he's the number-one feet maker in the country. Now every-

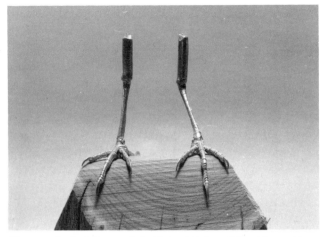

These meadowlark feet, made by Richard Delise of West Chester, Pennsylvania, are cast in pewter.

A woodcock and its cast feet.

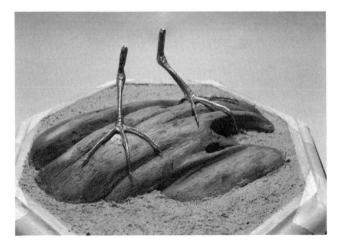

Cast woodcock feet.

A white-throated sparrow with cast feet.

body uses cast feet, except most of the professional carvers who put their stuff into competitions."

Though a number of carvers prefer to make their own feet, using wire in most cases with toes soldered to legs, competitions discourage others from using commercially made feet. Particularly for the World Championships, professional class, judges expect all of the bird and most of its habitat to be made by the carver. This explains why Ernie spent weeks carving a cow's skull instead of taking the one he had and putting it on the walnut base, and why he made stones and pebbles for it from putty. He did not, however, sculpt a branch out of artificial materials for the great horned owl, though he carved and shaped it to fit the dead quail.

"Now how can you tell the difference between cast

The old-time method of making feet was to take lead sheets and hammer them onto a piece of steel with the reverse impressions of the feet carved in.

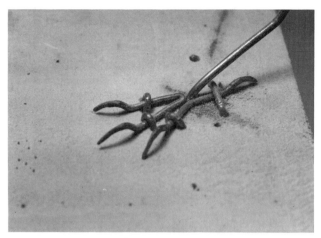

A contemporary method of making feet is to use copper wire soldered together. After the pieces of wire are joined, they can be given more detail. This technique was devised by bird carver Robert Guge of Carpentersville, Illinois.

Cast chickadee feet to be added to leg wire. Ernie says the leg wire can be made of material stronger than pewter to give more support to a heavy bird.

feet and something else? I guess if they're too good, they're cast feet. Cast feet usually have a seam in them where the molds were together, a flaring. Oh, you can tell.

A problem with cast feet is that they're not strong enough for songbirds. Ernie uses 18-gauge wire, flattened on an anvil. He then raps the wire with a cold chisel to create a tendon, or a lengthwise crease, running down the leg. The scales characteristic of a bird's leg and feet are made with a diamond cutter. And the feet are pewter. What he does so the bird is not standing on cast feet is have the leg wires hold the bird in place. They act like posts in the base or branch. The pewter castings then get butted up against the heavy wire and are simply glued in place, with the bird's back toe joined as a separate piece. Since these feet are weak, they can be bent to conform to the perch or base the bird is on. As Ernie puts it, "I don't have to worry about someone giving the bird a hit and having it sag."

Sagging is what happened with a shorebird he made, a yellowlegs. Its legs, being long and not strong enough to hold the weight of the bird, caused the body to sag. He had to create a small branch under the bird's belly to keep it from eventually falling over completely.

He puts more wash on the back of one of the chickadees. "When I was a little kid, I carried a notebook around in my pocket, and whenever I had a thought about something, a solution to some problem, I would jot it down in my idea book. That's what led me to do those articles for *Popular Science.* I had invented a couple of different greenhouses, a ski tow. I guess I

This lesser yellowlegs was too heavy to be supported by its cast legs, so Ernie used part of the driftwood to support the chest of the bird.

But many of the castings will be sufficient to hold the bird, as with these robin's feet and legs.

invented the first way I used to paint on smooth birds. It was a mixture of washes and matte medium to get the porcelain look those original birds had during the first ten years I was carving. Then I got Rick Delise set up with pewter feet, and then I started burning for color. And around that time, I helped introduce ruby carvers."

High-speed bits with differently shaped heads impregnated with ruby grit, these cutters came directly from the dental industry. Made in Europe, they grind away material, leaving a fairly smooth surface. Ernie describes them as a major breakthrough for carving birds, as was the Foredom. Before that, steel cutters were "chattery" on the surface of the wood, leaving dig marks rather than a smooth surface. He relates how they came to be used by most carvers for doing muscles and bumps or even finer details, or for undercutting an area like a wing.

"A doctor who carves birds was in a couple of my classes. He was very interested in new things. Maybe five years ago he ran across these ruby carvers in a dental catalog. He ran them up to me and said I should try them. I guess what he gave me were barrel-shaped, rounded-off cylinders. I thought they worked really great, but nobody had seen them. I was using jelutong roughed out with Arco rotary rasps and finished with knife work on the wings, the tail, the beak.

"I did a seminar out in San Francisco and demonstrated to the class how to work ruby carvers on a quail. There was a guy in the class who was selling carving supplies, and he thought they were really great. I told him there was a company on Long Island that sold them." He pauses. "It's funny how this went from the East Coast to the West Coast and back again."

That same doctor has brought Ernie different bits impregnated with diamond grit. "Every time he brings me something, it changes the appearance of my birds," Ernie says, setting a chickadee in front of the hair-dryer and going to the other table to bring back the diamond-covered grinding bits. Some are extremely fine. One is spear-shaped and ends in a sharp tip; another is pear-shaped. He picks that one up from its holder and says, "This one I use for doing little details around the nostrils and eyes. The very fine pointed one I can use for making feathers on the head. You know, every time I pick up one of these, I wonder how I got along without it."

He removes a barrel-shaped stone from the holder. "I ground the end off this one to make feather separa-

Ernie was instrumental in introducing ruby carvers to bird carvers. Doing details such as those shown here was difficult before these bits were available.

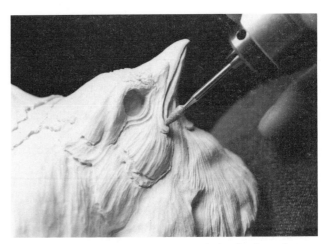

One of the ruby carvers available today can do fine details on the anatomy of a bird. Ernie is working on the mouth of a baby bluejay.

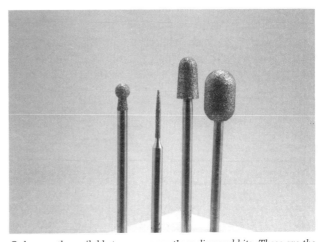

Only recently available to carvers are these diamond bits. These are the ones Ernie uses most frequently. Very fine detailing or sanding can be done with them. Ernie says they are particularly effective in a high-speed grinder that runs at 30,000 rpm or better.

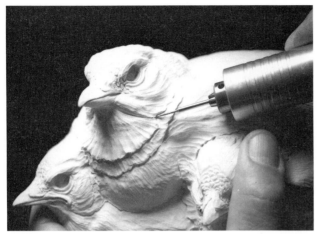

Ernie uses a needle-pointed diamond bit to undercut fine or small feathers.

The results of feather layering on the back of a mother bluejay.

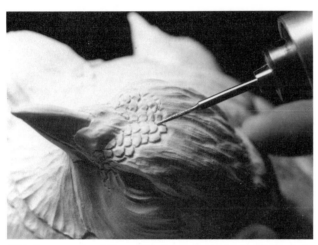

With the same pointed diamond bit, he can put feathers on the head of a bird.

Despite the diamond bits, Ernie still uses the ruby carvers to do most of the fine work on his birds. Here he has ground flat the end of a ruby carver and uses it to layer wing feathers.

This black-necked stilt, made from a piece of tupelo, was done almost entirely with ruby carvers. The legs are positioned in such a way that a bandsaw could not get between them. This wood was removed with a ruby carver.

tions, layering the feathers. I also run it down either side of the feather quill to raise it. And I can stone in detail on the breast with it. These diamond cutters are fairly new. They run about $10, $12 apiece. The ruby carvers run $5, $6, $7 each."

Ruby carvers and diamond bits also helped Ernie make the transition from jelutong to tupelo, although his first piece of Louisiana swamp wood was not workable. That was about three years ago, before the great horned owl. "I tried to make some chickadees, but it was a bad piece—too hard, too dense. It was like working with a piece of rubber. I couldn't make a dent with a Foredom tool. And everybody was telling me to use tupelo." The next piece he got was from Phil English, whose P.C. English Enterprises is known as a major supplier of carving accessories. That piece,

Ernie says, was beautiful, though he can't remember whether he made a woodcock or a bobwhite quail from it.

The tool dealers respond quickly to the needs of the carvers. A carver turns up a bit that can raise feathers on the forehead of a bird and within a year a dozen catalogs make available diamond-tipped cutters with a tip less than $1/16$ inch in diameter.

"Working tupelo is like working something that is not wood, plastic, soap, I don't know what. It's not fibery. It's the most unwoodlike wood you can think of. There's no sap, no smell. It's strong, but it turns to powder with a ruby carver or other cutter. And with the end grain, you can take a piece of it and almost tie a knot in it, it's so flexible. It's a strange wood, but I love it."

The stilt is made from one piece of tupelo with no inserts.

The finished stilt, burned and painted.

Another view of the black-necked stilt.

Before ruby carvers and the Foredom tool, Ernie did much of his carving with a knife. Here he was working on a chickadee in his first studio, part of which is still a farm stand.

Because of its sometimes spongy nature, tupelo resists knife work. But that doesn't bother Ernie. He describes knives as cumbersome, slow. And on another species of wood, he would have to worry about splitting if he went against the grain. "With knife work, you have to be dead sure how you lay out your pattern. And it's just primitive. Guys who use them don't like to hear that. Maybe they think it's more aesthetic with knives, more pleasing than working with the screaming Foredom tool that gets dust up your nose. But if you have to do this to make a living, you have to do it as fast as possible. The end of knives for me was when I discovered ruby carvers."

Ernie had recently finished a piece made up of a mother blue jay and three baby birds under her body and wings. It was made possible by the wood, tupelo, and the ruby carvers and diamond bits. He says he made one attempt at doing it seven years ago. The attempt is behind his painting area. The wood is roughly shaped; the mother's head is too far removed from the babies' heads, which themselves have noticeable gaps between them.

He had seen a photograph in a *National Wildlife* magazine of the mother and her young in a nest. Seven years later, he decided to make another try. He says he designed two patterns, one for the mother, another for the babies, and neither one a side profile. And, like the owl, three attempts were made before he brought it successfully out of the wood. "I started whacking away at it, but one of the babies was too far in, so I had to discard that. For the second piece I used jelutong because I didn't have any tupelo. I had it all roughed out and put it away, went to the house for dinner, came back the next morning, and it had a crack right across the back. That was the end of that piece." For the third piece, he purchased tupelo from Phil English. That came out fine, he says.

Ernie points out that with the tupelo, "I could have laid out the pattern for the jays any old way on the wood and it wouldn't have made a bit of difference whether I was working crossgrain, up, down, or sideways. With jelutong, I had to worry about the beaks breaking off and favoring the grain."

He talks more about the patterns for the blue jay family, saying that a side profile was impossible because the birds were arranged in a slight semicircle. Getting the general outline was first: Ernie started with a piece of wood 5 inches thick, 9 inches wide, and 12 inches long. He took ½ inch off most of the bottom, however, so that the tail feathers dipped

Ernie calls this the original false start on the blue jay family done seven years ago. Made from jelutong, the piece was worked with carbide cutters.

The inspiration for the blue jay family came from a photo in National Wildlife *magazine.*

With ruby carvers, Ernie was able to make this blue jay family in 1985.

What also made the blue jay family possible was the use of tupelo. Still, it was a difficult piece to carve since a side profile pattern could not be used.

lower than the flat bottom of the birds. He says it was just something to do. "I thought the tail would look good hanging over the edge of the base. It added dimension to the piece."

He remembers shaping the birds, beginning with the mother's head. Then he measured the distance between the top of the head of the mother and the middle baby. He cut that wood away, and he did the same for the other two. He made a general side view and cut out the excess for each bird. "I got all the heads in first and worked my way out. Once I got the heads and eyes and beaks in, I got an idea of the placement of everything else.

"It was kind of hard to get everything to fit. I had to ask myself where one body ended and another began. And then I wondered where I should stop carving so I

What also made this a difficult piece was the way the baby blue jays fit under and against the mother bird. Overlapping feathers helped with the transitions.

To do a cluster of four baby chickadees, Ernie started with the top bird's head. He followed the same strategy with the blue jay family.

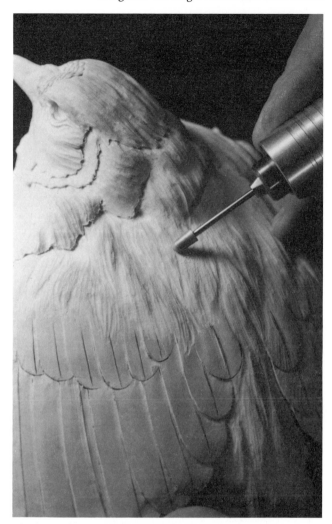

The carved cluster.

The diamond bits not only lend themselves to fine detailing but also to sanding a surface. This leaves smooth, though irregular hills and valleys on the bird, as is shown on the back of the mother jay and baby birds composition. A sanded-flat surface would make for a hard rather than a soft look when the paint is applied.

would have enough for a chest or a cheek. I had to visualize what I was doing and hope that I didn't cut away too much." He summarizes. "I guess I started from high spots and worked in the way a sculptor would." He adds that there is a design to the grouping that he calls "that old circular design. It goes around and around. It has a nice flow to it."

Fine detailing with ruby carvers and diamond bits was not the only work he did. "Recently," he explains, "I've been going over a bird with a little ball-shaped diamond cutter to sand it. I went over the whole owl with that bit," he says without reviewing any of the frustrations. "And I went over the bluejays bit by bit, feather by feather, covering 1/16 inch at a time. It takes as long to sand it this way as it does to burn a bird."

What the small ball bit does is remove pieces of wood grain sticking up, even on the microscopic level. At the same time it leaves a variety of minute, albeit smooth, grooves. Ernie describes these grooves as planes. "When burned and painted, the bird gives the appearance of having soft feathers because you're seeing a surface that varies in depth, maybe only 1/16 of an inch."

He compares the ball-shaped diamond bit to using 150- to 200-grit sandpaper, a ruby carver to 75- or 100-grit paper. "Working the bird over with 150-grit is really fine enough," Ernie says of the sanding process. "Actually, the burning has some kind of sanding effect that helps smooth out imperfections, blending them into the bird. The main thing is not to have any fuzz.

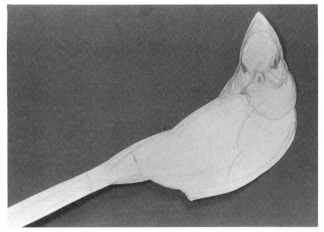

Ernie demonstrates his tools and techniques on this adult blue jay. This is the pattern he started with.

A cylinder-shaped diamond bit sands the back of the bird.

Ruby carvers have done much of the shaping on the blue jay's head.

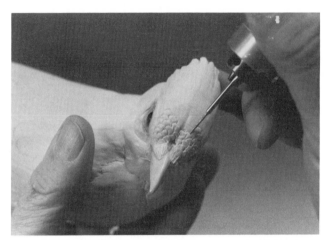

A needle-pointed diamond bit cuts in the head feathers.

"The reason for not using sandpaper is that it leaves a flat surface. You don't have any of those high spots." He rubs a finger lightly across the back of one of the chickadees, noting that he can feel minute grooves. "With the diamond bit, you make a lot of small depressions or planes in the same direction as the feather barbs. If the feathers were perfectly flat before I burned them, they would look flat. But now they have ridges. You have variations in depth, which give a softness to the bird."

He describes soft and hard surfaces to carry the explanation further. "Why does velvet or hair look soft? It's because you're focusing on different depths. A piece of granite looks hard because you don't have that. It's the same with a feather that's not been made absolutely smooth by sanding it. You're looking down into depths. That's why you know these chickadees

The head at this stage.

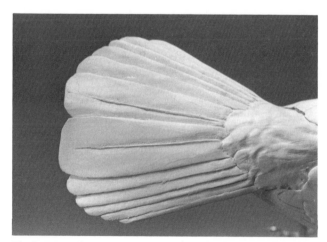

The same bit slightly undercuts the chest feathers.

Tail feathers can actually be separated using a small circular saw blade in the Foredom.

More undercutting on the chest feathers.

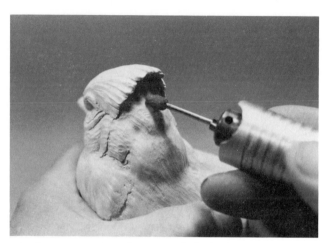

A ruby carver can shape the crest on the back of the blue jay's head.

The layering of the tail feathers and their quills is done with ruby carvers.

Not all sanding is done with a diamond bit. Some areas Ernie does want smooth. Here he uses a piece of sandpaper wrapped around a spindle.

More sanding with 280-grit wet/dry sandpaper.

More burning on the cheeks with feather breaks put in with the pen.

A light burn using a tight tip is done on the head of the blue jay.

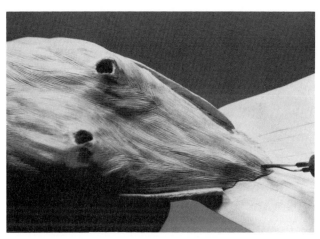

Making a loose, hairy effect on under-tail coverts with a light burn.

A skew tip and a high heat setting puts in the dark feather patterns.

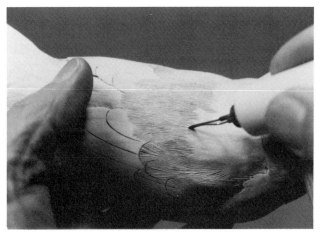

There is also a hairy look on the back of the bird. This is an area where feathers are not defined but blend together as clumps.

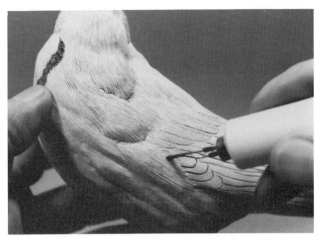

Working on the breast feathers with a light burn.

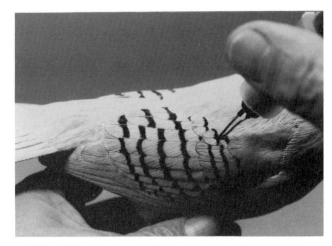

Doing the bars on the secondary coverts with a high heat setting.

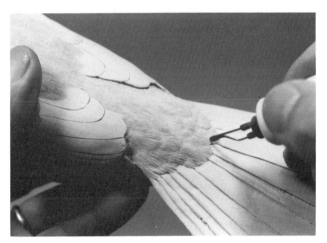

The rump of the bird starts to show individual feathers.

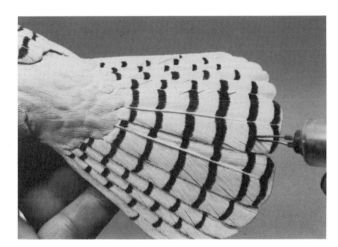

Putting the dark patterns on the tail feathers.

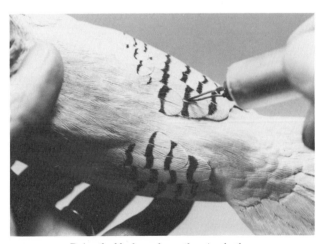

Doing the black marks on the wing feathers.

The painted bird, which ended up as a wall mount.

Mixes of ultramarine blue and burnt umber did most of the blues on the bird. Prior washes of gesso created the white on the bird, though they were toned down with washes of burnt umber.

The back of the immature chickadees. Ernie points out that some areas will reflect light while others won't, depending on what was sanded. The breasts, for example, were sanded with a diamond bit to enhance a soft look.

Another shot of the fully painted bird.

To get some reflected light off the wings, sandpaper is used to get a smooth surface.

have feathers and are not made of stone. Light rays come back at different lengths. And it may only be a matter of a millimeter that makes the difference."

Ernie says this varying of depth explains why so little reflective light comes off his birds. "You don't see high spots or highlights. I think that, too, makes for that soft look. Even if you put on too much undercoating, you'll get too much of the same depth that will reflect light." In contrast, however, he makes a bill very smooth with 600-grit sandpaper, giving it a boney, hard look. And he will do some sanding on tail feathers. He puts a finger on the tail of a chickadee. "Throw a light on these feathers and you'll see some light coming off them. That's the way they should look naturally."

By contrast, the rump of this bird was gone over with a diamond bit, while the tail was gone over with sandpaper.

He remembers that the blue jay mother had some reflective light on the primaries, the result of sanding with paper, but none on the secondaries. He concludes, "Where you want light to reflect, you sandpaper. Parts that you don't want to reflect light you go over with a ruby carver or a diamond bit and keep those varying depths, hills and valleys. You want that roughness in there."

Putting his brush into a can of water, he says, "The faster these ruby carvers and diamond bits go, the better they cut." That makes the Foredom tool, which rotates a bit at 14,000 rpm, too slow. New machines are coming on the market that double and triple that speed. Ernie has just purchased a grinding tool with a lightweight handpiece that has a simple cord instead of a flexible shaft and runs at 30,000 rpm. Another tool recently available to carvers runs at 45,000 rpm.

"It goes on and on," he says, looking out the window into the dimming light of late afternoon. "But how far can it go? Can the birds look any more real?" He shakes his head slightly. "The thing to do now is emphasize design."

The Teacher

"Look at the softness of these little guys. Don't they just turn you on?" he says, as if he has made a revelation to himself. He turns off the switch of the hairdryer with a slow, heavy finality and leans back on his stool. The softness of the birds is apparent; the colors combine with burning and bumps to create the look of a Muehlmatt bird; the grays and blacks of the chickadees reflect little light as Ernie has already pointed out.

"Do you see what this muted palette can do?" he asks, as he lifts one of the birds from its branch. Returning it to its perch, he says, "That's always something I like to get across to my students." He explains a strategy he used when he taught a one-week seminar sponsored by the Ward Foundation and held at the Salisbury State College. "Before I started painting the meadowlark I brought along, I showed the class the three skins I had with me. I asked everybody what color he saw in the bird." He pauses with a smile. "Everybody started shouting out, 'I see burnt umber,' or 'I see raw umber,' or 'I see yellow ochre.' Meanwhile, I was writing these colors down. I had a whole list of them." His hands pantomime note-taking. "I wanted to

show the students that you can paint without any stress and strain and worry. So I said, 'Let's pick a color.' I made a mix of burnt umber and slopped it on the bird. I said to the class, 'What do you think?' They said 'too brown.'"

He sits upright and continues. "I explained the color wheel to them, and they said, 'Add ultramarine blue.' So I slopped that on. 'How's that?' I asked. They were having a ball. It kept on like that while I pretended I didn't know what I was doing." His tone is more serious now. "But you see, you couldn't mess up the bird because you just neutralize one color with another color. When they saw how I goofed up and then made corrections, they lost all their fear of painting. And that was the point I was trying to get across." He spaces out his words now. "Just make your washes light enough. Never put them on so thick that they scream at you."

He recalls another seminar. This time it was for the Easton, Maryland, Waterfowl Festival. "They made this videotape." He lifts himself stiffly out of the stool. "Let's take a look at it," he says, adding that he himself has only seen a few minutes of the tape.

Ernie in his studio with carving students. Dr. Louis Iozzi, on the far left, introduced Ernie to ruby carvers.

Ernie calls this a great profile shot of a bobwhite quail head. Photo by Larry Stevens. *(See appendix for address.)*

It's over two hundred brisk steps from the bottom of the shop stairs past the greenhouse with its exhaust fan blades invisibly at work, past a European larch, past the in-ground swimming pool and the dog that waits in summer for a buoyant tennis ball to float to its edge, to the ranch-style house. Inside he has collected decoys that sit on shelves placed above the windows of a converted porch. Below them are wildfowl prints by Don Whitlach and Arthur Singer.

In the living room, the title appears in capitals on the screen: "The Waterfowl Festival First Masters Carving Seminar." Ernie has found a seat at the edge of a church auditorium stage. He wears his sweater, the one with the Wild Wings Decoy Den insignia, its sleeves pushed up nearly to his elbows. His look is somber as if affected by the building, but he claims later that he is nervous in front of an audience.

That he has brought his own props is obvious. There's a stool from his shop, a Foredom on an intravenous stand, a Diastar slide viewer, blocks of partially carved wood, mounted birds, and a music stand.

"How many have carved a bird before?" he asks. Without waiting to take count, he asks, "How many people have trouble painting?" The response is laughter. "I enjoy the painting and the burning. They're my two favorite things. I don't know how I got stuck with the carving." More laughter eddys through the auditorium, and it enables him to make a smooth transition to what he came to teach.

"When I do a bird I try to get all the research material I can have. From skins, you can get bill sizes, the length of the wings and tail, and body sizes. And get as many pictures as you can." He walks to a table where

he indicates two stuffed and mounted quail.

Walking to the music stand, he removes a black and white photo of a bobwhite quail. He describes the photos. "This fellow Larry Stevens sells these. I have a right- and left-head profile and a couple of color shots showing the breast pattern and other colors."

He moves a few feet to his right to the slide viewer. "I have this projector so you can show slides as you're working." He has photographed a bobwhite quail in two dozen stages of work, from rough-shaping to the finished game bird. He claims he forgets after some six months how to do a bobwhite quail. "So I drag out these slides. They're especially helpful in the burning and painting end of it." He does not add that he has carved over one hundred bobwhite quail.

A slide appears. On a thick piece of wood is the top profile of a bird, its head turned to the left. That it is a quail body is unmistakable. He suddenly looks annoyed, as if the wrong slide came into view. Before he slides another into place, he looks at his watch. "Let's get into this. We're running a little late.

"You make your side profile first," he says rapidly. "But a lot of you have trouble drawing." He moves back to the table and picks up what appears to be a pattern for a quail. "So I came up with this thing, a little manikin," he says, as he holds up an articulated cardboard quail body. He explains that there are only five movable parts on a bird's body, as he moves quickly to a blackboard and fingers a piece of chalk with his free hand. "The body never moves. It's like an egg," he says, as the board accepts a large oval shape. But he points out that quails are really melon-shaped. "The other movable parts are the neck, the head, the rump, and the tail. You can get any number of different positions. You can get an alert bird or a sleeping bird, just by jiggling this thing around." He demonstrates, twisting the head upward, turning the tail downward. Redrawing the front of the bird oval, he indicates that the breast also moves—but only in and out.

Someone in the audience asks how the manikin was made. "Just little bolts," Ernie answers.

Not to let the audience think he does birds with inserts and separate heads, he says, "Ninety-nine percent of my birds are one piece—except a woodcock or an avocet; then I add the bill.

"But if you have problems doing a bird like this one with the head sideways, it might be helpful to carve one bird, cut the head off, and turn it as a model for the next one. You're only wasting an hour, and you avoid this agony of trying to cover up the seam line." He puts the manikin down and lifts off the table two roughly shaped quail bodies with their heads turned to one side. He holds them up, one in each hand.

"Let me show you how to turn the head without changing the pattern." Perhaps afraid he will forget to tell the audience later, Ernie says, "Take advantage of the grain." He holds up another block with a side profile drawn in pencil. An arrow on the lower right is drawn with its head pointing down. "I want the strength in the tail. It facilitates burning when you have the grain running the way you burn. Sometimes when you burn crossgrain, it gets torn up a little bit. It's not as slick and neat," he says.

He puts that block down and picks up still another block of wood, this one partially sawn to shape. He explains that he laid the pattern on the wood and cut around it to get a side profile. "Now I want to turn the head 45 degrees. I got the centerline down the back of the bird and drew a top profile. It's fairly egg-shaped, so you can always take the side width and transfer it to the top," he explains as his hands make broad gestures around the wood.

"I drew the beak in as if the bird were looking straight ahead." He demonstrates how he has found where the neck meets the body on the side. "Run a line up and across the top of the bird." At the intersection of that line and the body's centerline he has made an X. This will be where he will put a compass point. This should also be the highest point on the upright bird's head. But first he shows that he has drawn a straight-on head on the top of the wood.

He has taken a compass from the table. "So I put my compass on that point, and that's where I'm going to arc off the beak," from its tip and from where the beak meets the forehead. The wood has two arcs darkly drawn and a new beak, some 45 degrees right of center, penciled in. "Then I make a new centerline." He adds, parenthetically, "I think the top profile is tough to come up with."

He shifts the block from his right to his left hand and picks up another quail profile, this one with more wood removed. "Now you're going to come up with a funny-looking head," after the turned head has been bandsawed. "There are going to be high parts, but you can nip that extra wood off with the bandsaw." The bandsaw blade cannot compensate for the turn of the head and the fact that the forehead slopes at an angle different from the body. Instead, it responds to pattern

If Ernie were to make a jointed model of a bobwhite quail, the penciled dots would indicate where the flexible joints would be.

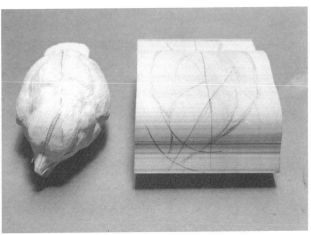

This is how Ernie turns the head of a bird, as he did with this chickadee.

A bobwhite quail with a turned head and the original centerline. This centerline should not be ground away during the rough shaping.

A mounted bobwhite quail, one Ernie describes as "not too great."

lines that would seem to indicate the entire bird has been flattened out. What results is a corner of the head higher on the side the head is turned toward. "I always hold the bird up and look at it straight on," he says, and does so with the body block. "It's a little tricky, but after you do a few it becomes easy. Cut a little bit under the chin to depress that area and a little bit on the side to depress that area," he says, making chopping motions with the edge of one hand.

He reflects for a moment. He says he has at home a ¾ horsepower bench motor with a large rotary rasp attachment. The bandsaw and the rasp remove 90 percent of the wood. He holds up another bird, shaped and rounded but without details. "The time to lay out your pattern on the wood and cut it and round it off is about fifteen minutes." His free hands describe circles and pirouettes around the wood.

He picks his glasses up off the table and puts them on, then reaches for a pair of large cast feet. "Pick up the legs you're going to use and hold them under the bird to see whether you're too far forward or back and drill holes for them." He indicates that holes are already in the latest body block. "If you wait too long, you could have everything off."

Telling the audience that he obtained these cast feet from Rick Delise and that competition birds have to have feet shaped by the carver, he continues, "To determine where the legs go, hold the bird up in the position it's going to be standing in. Hold the legs where they look good." He demonstrates by holding a leg against the side of the body. "This is obviously too far front; this, too far back."

He has brought along a base, a piece of cedar flattened on its bottom. The cast feet have pegs, he points out, and he assembles bird, feet, and legs. The quail, though only naked wood, has a definably alert look. "See how it looks. Bend it forward or backward," he says, moving the bird slightly to demonstrate how the attitude of the bird changes as its pose changes.

"Next is carving the head. I start with the beak and work back to the cheeks, the cape, the tail and go to the next phase."

He directs the audience back to one of his mounted birds. "Be careful of mounted birds. Just because it's mounted, it doesn't mean it's good. Actually a mounted bird is a skin and whatever the taxidermist decided to stuff it with." He takes his calipers and pantomimes a measurement over the head.

He comments on the carved bird. "If the head looks good and the eyes are set right, the rest usually look

A preening bobwhite quail that was used as the model for one of the birds in Ernie's Needles, Feathers, and Bone *composition.*

good. You never get by with a bird with a bad head and a good body. If the head comes off good, you can overlook lots of mistakes on the body. The head is what people look at first."

He is ready to start grinding with the Foredom. "I'm going to make the depressions for the eyes." He puts the calipers over the mounted quail head to take a measurement and says, "This bird has a pretty good head."

Seated on his stool, his foot on the control pedal of the Foredom tool, he says, "I use a ruby carver for this part. They come in all different shapes and sizes. I start with a barrel shape, then a pear shape, and work toward smaller sizes." He holds up the bits.

Someone asks where they can be bought. He indicates that dealers set up for that weekend are selling them. "Or if you have a dental supply place in your town, you can pretend you're a dentist."

The bird propped on one knee, his foot running the machine with its flexible shaft, he says, "I'm going to depress the area under the bill. These ruby carvers are great. They pulverize the wood." He says he is using jelutong, not knowing he will permanently switch to tupelo in a few months. "Ruby carvers eat into the wood without any pressure and leave almost a sanded surface. Jelutong's a wood from Malaysia." The ruby carver rises and lowers in a grinding pitch as he presses into the wood.

As a thin layer of sawdust collects on his pants, Ernie says, "It doesn't take too much. You can usually burn and paint without too much concentration, but to get the bird carved properly takes more concentration." He talks as if conversing with himself. He ad-

vises against listening to talk radio, "But you can listen to music. Burning is a good daydreaming occupation. Painting is very easy for me," he says above the sound of ruby carver pulverizing wood.

Holding the bird up, he says, "I keep looking at it from the side. We're getting a halfway decent profile." He adds that he restores the centerline if it gets ground away, "so I can keep the head symmetrical.

"The next thing I do is get the top profile of just the beak. Notice where it meets the head. I'll use another ruby carver with a bevel on it. You don't have to watch your angle of attack so carefully." Holding the quail head against his leg, he uses the ruby carver to work wood away from the top of the bill at an angle. "To get a bobwhite quail ready for burning would take about a day," he tells the audience.

He holds up the bird again. "You could draw in where the bill separation is to guide you. I don't do that, but it might be helpful." He compares a quail's beak to a kestrel's, noting that it ends in a hook. "Look at the pictures to see how the beak hangs down considerably. A hawky-type beak."

He releases his foot from the pedal. "OK, that's enough on the beak. The next thing would be to determine what width you want between the eyes. I'll take it off this mount," he says, moving to the table. "Make it so your calipers run right through. The glass eye will stick out just a little bit from the depression." He adjusts the calipers this time, carefully. "One inch. That's good. I do this by looking at the bird head on," he adds as he returns to his Foredom station.

"I start where the upper and lower bill come to-

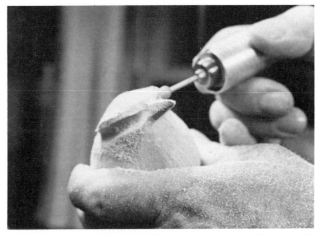

After the initial roughing, one of the first areas to be worked on is the eye channels. These Ernie makes with a ruby carver. Photo courtesy of Wildfowl Carving and Collecting.

Details on a bobwhite quail head.

Ernie says that all muscles and bumps are camouflaged by the burning and painting. Photo courtesy of Wildfowl Carving and Collecting

gether and work up in an arc." He draws in a line across the face. He has also put a different ruby carver into the Foredom handpiece. "I use this pear-shaped ruby carver." He notes how little sawdust is actually made by the ruby carvers. "They don't throw sawdust all over the place."

"That chattering noise you hear is when I get in too tight. These ruby carvers never wear out. The only thing that can happen is they can snap off at the chuck from fatigue." As he says this, he lays the ruby carver on its edge and begins routing out an eye channel.

Without stopping the Foredom, he continues, "I do the same procedure for any bird I'm doing, working from the beak on back." He brings the calipers back to the head and tells the audience that the eye channels still jut out by ⅛ inch too much.

He seems to get ahead of himself when he says, "A great thing to do is exaggerate every detail on the bird. I'll exaggerate the puffiness around the cheeks." A pause. "I exaggerate every feather group. The chest. On the back. After you paint and burn, it all flattens out." He tells the audience to stop and look at his display table where he has a finished woodcock and quail. "You would swear they were perfectly flat, but run your finger over the areas. They're as bumpy as can be."

He checks the channels one more time with the calipers. He goes to the slide viewer and moves another slide into place. It's a quail at the same stage as the model he is working on. "There's the depression on the eyes. Now I'll round the head off." Back at the blackboard he draws a circle for the quail's head and makes indentations on either side to show the eye

channels. He points out the sharp edges left at the tops of the depressions, calling them sharp angles. He adds, "I'm going to round them right off."

Back at the Foredom, Ernie says a common mistake for beginning carvers is allowing the glass eyes to bulge out. He advises looking at the top of the carved bird, "like this one here," he says. "After the eyes are set in, very little of the glass should be visible if the bird is looked at from above." He peeks with an exaggerated, bug-eyed stare over the tops of his glasses as he says this. "It's a very common mistake. I did it myself in the beginning," he adds as if to pacify those who make bug-eyed wildfowl.

Again using the edge of the ruby carver to "brush" away wood from above the eyes, he says, "These cutters are not the fastest things in the world, but they're very accurate, and it's hard to make a mistake."

He decides to comment about the wood. "Jelutong doesn't have any fiber. No hair the way basswood has." A question from the audience. A man asks how jelutong carves with a knife. "It's not as strong as basswood," Ernie answers. "You have to be very careful of its splintering. But with a Foredom, it doesn't really matter. You can get quite thin areas, and it will hold up."

Still running the Foredom, he says, "Can you see how this wood almost disappears in front of your eyes? It's a lot of fun working with this jelutong." Another question: Is jelutong difficult to find? "Someone here is probably selling it. I live right outside of Philadelphia and a large lumber company halfway between there and Wilmington [Delaware] sells it. The guy who runs it is a duck carver. It runs between $2.00

and $2.50 a board foot. It's all kiln-dried. There's no moisture in it.

"Now what's next?" he asks as he puts down the Foredom and goes to the slide viewer, moving the next slide, showing a quail, into place. Pointing out the area under the quail's chin, he says of it, "It's not really defined on the bird, but I'm going to puff it out a little bit. I could use a pencil [to draw it in], but I'll use the Foredom tool as my pencil." Back with the Foredom, he says, "You can use your imagination with these bumps. I put them in a different spot every time. Whatever turns you on." A pause. "As long as it looks good."

A few minutes later, it's back to the music stand and the photos. He points to one. "Usually the front of the eye is in a line from the beginning of the beak. Check the photo for how far back," he says, and picks up a pencil. He holds his quail so that its right side faces him and draws a circle for the eye. "Do the right eye first," he says, pointing out that he is right-handed. "Look straight ahead to make sure the eyes are at the same level, not one higher than the other." He explains that if he did the left eye first, he would have to wrap his right hand around the bird to draw in the left eye as he holds the bird facing him. "And check from the top so one eye is not too far in toward the beak." As he demonstrates, he says that one eye is too far forward. He is so casual about it, he might have planned it that way.

Telling the audience that the quail requires an 8-millimeter eye, Ernie slips a brass band around the Foredom. It holds a glass eye and its customary length of wire molded into its back. It sticks out into space like a disembodied eye from a horror movie. He ex-

plains his small invention. "I can check for the right depth without having to put down the Foredom." He continues that he uses a small, pear-shaped cutter to bore out the eyehole. "It's a matter of wearing away the wood so the eye is flush with the wood. Then when you clip the wire and reverse the glass, it will be the right depth." As the ruby carver makes a hole, he says, "Check, go back, check, go back, check, go back." A minute later, as he pokes the glass eye into the hole, he says, "See how that eye just disappears?"

After a few moments filled with the sound of the Foredom and ruby carver hitting high and low pitches, he asks, "Does that noise from the Foredom tool bother you? Some people come into my studio and say it sounds like a dentist's [drill]. I never noticed that it bothered me."

He explains that he will create an indentation from

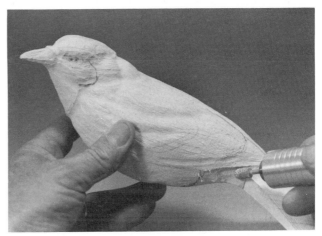

Ernie will use a carbide cutter for a large bird like this bluejay. The cutter will remove more wood faster than a ruby carver can.

Instead of using a knife, fine detail can be achieved with ruby carvers and even a burning pen tip.

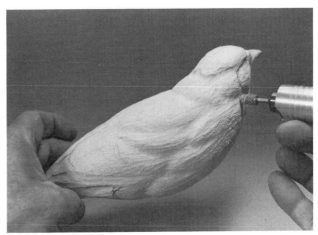

Working around the head with the carbide cutter.

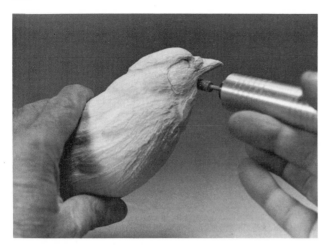

Establishing the side profile.

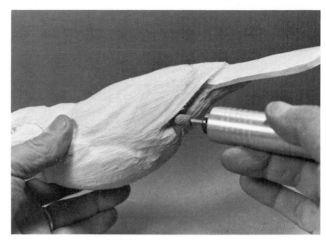

Undercutting the wing of the bluejay.

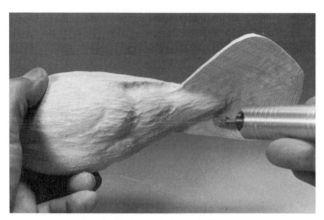

Rough-shaping with the carbide cutter.

the corners of the eyes to the beak, and "put a little bag under the eyes. Whatever you do, it flattens out in the long run." He creates a depression over one eye. Now do the same thing on the other side, using the Foredom as you would a pencil," he says, blowing dust off the quail's face.

"She's shaping up," he shares with the audience before he goes to the music stand and the Larry Stevens profile photo of a quail. "See how the beak comes back into the head. Half the beak goes back into the head on a quail." He uses his pencil as a pointer and runs it along the picture. "Especially when you're doing birds with an open mouth," he adds. After a minute of work with the Foredom, he has flared the beak into the head. "Little baby chickadees have a lot of wrinkles under the eyes. "I'll put a few wrinkles around the eye for you."

"What is a ruby carver?" someone finally asks. "It's a metal rod covered with little tiny bits of ruby. You can do a lot of fun things with a ruby carver," Ernie answers.

He next creates a depression at the top of the beak. "I just jam it in," he explains, "to make the areas for the nostrils." But the nostrils themselves, as well as the beak separation, he will make with a cool burning pen. He underlines cool with his voice. The beak, he says, can be gone over with the pear-shaped ruby carver to create the illusion of overlapping mandibles. "When you burn a line, it helps to guide your tool so it doesn't jump around."

Someone calls out that only five minutes are left. Ernie checks his watch. "As far as the rest of the bird goes, I would go back to a carbide cutter. It's faster and rougher going." He hunts for it on the table. "I would draw with that," he says, holding it up. "I shape the cape with it. I make a depression with it." He talks quickly about making feather groups. "Make a hump by making a depression all the way around with the Foredom and rounding it off," he says of the wings. A small hollow above the depressions make for wings tucked in; a slight hollow below makes for slightly raised ones. "Keep the upper part rounded," he says, gesturing with his fingers curled toward his face.

"I feel like I didn't cover a heck of a lot. Yes," he responds to a man in the audience, "there's a finished bird on the table at the armory, a nicely finished bobwhite almost in this position. I hope you had a good time. Thank you."

Part Two:
The Projects

Black-capped Chickadee

Adult Chickadee

The pattern with the study skin. This side profile is the exact size needed. When the bird is cut out and shaped with grinders, no wood should be removed from its length or width. In fact, the centerline, if drawn, should be there when all the rough carving is completed.

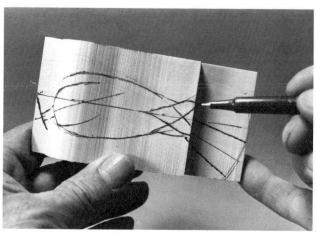

Cut out on the bandsaw as close to the outline as possible, leaving no excess wood anywhere; ⅛ inch left all the way around can end up as ¼ inch added to the anatomy, which is particularly bad for a small bird. Leaving extra wood in anticipation of a mistake later on is not a good strategy.

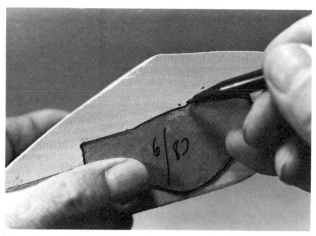

Trace the pattern onto a block of tupelo with a marking pencil. This is an old pattern, but one improved many times.

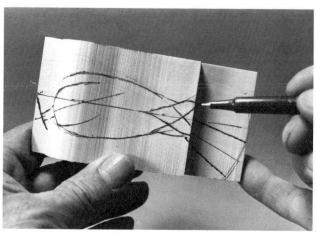

Draw in the top profile. The tail is swung to the left and the crossed wings are drawn in. The right wing will overlap the left wing. The head is also swung around. A compass is used to turn the anatomy and a new centerline is drawn for the head and tail.

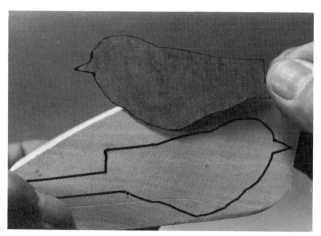

The pattern has been traced.

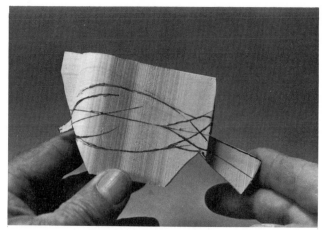

The first cuts are made with the bandsaw. First, cut in on either side of the bill, then go in perpendicular or at right angles to it and remove that wood. Do the same for the tail.

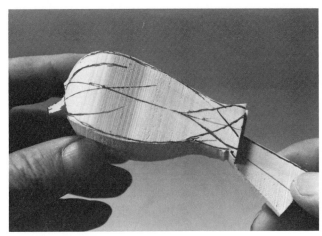

Run the bandsaw around the body from the wings up to the head, following the pattern.

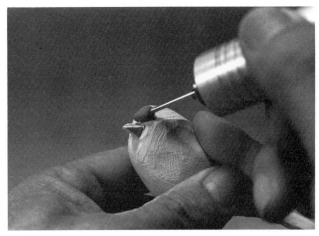

Define the bill and side profile of the head with a number 23 pear-shaped ruby carver, while disregarding the top profile.

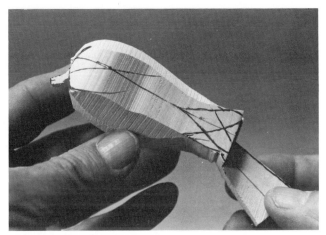

Round off the corners with the bandsaw. Let the bandsaw remove as much wood as possible.

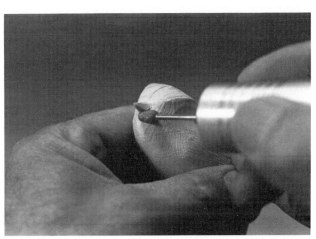

Working underneath the bill, remove some of the wood and establish the planes on the bill. Its shape is roughly like a pyramid, with two planes on top, three planes on the bottom.

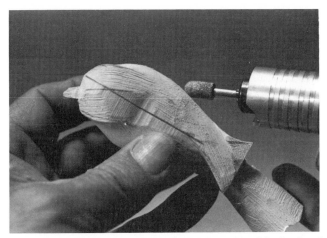

A carbide cutter in a Foredom tool defines the width of the head and rounds off the body, which is almost perfectly circular through the chest area. Notice that the centerline is still there. Work from that down each side. Do some shaping on the primaries, and do some slight rounding on the tail.

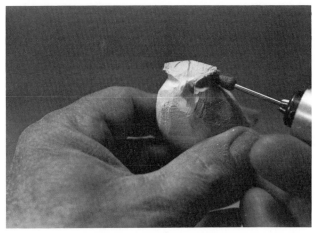

Make the eye depressions. To establish the width between the eyes, Ernie suggests you use your imagination. A stuffed chickadee gives only the measurement made by a taxidermist. But he estimates that it might be ¾ inch between the eyes.

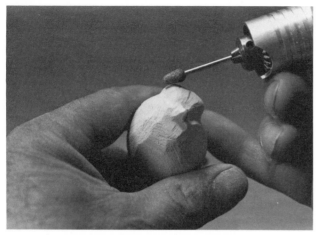

Round off the top of the head. Remove the overhanging brow, still using the pear-shaped ruby carver, but leave a flat area where the eyes are going to be put in. Notice again that the centerline still has not been ground or carved away.

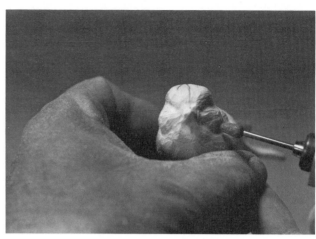

A front view of the cheeks. Note that they project about ⅛ inch beyond the eye channels, but they are not to be made too puffy, *Ernie cautions.*

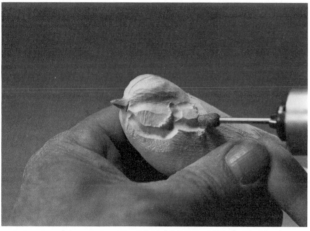

Define the cheeks. Draw them in with a pencil or a ruby carver while it's cutting, slowly increasing the depth until it is ⅛ inch. Ernie describes this as just a little valley for the cheek and the Muehlmatt bump behind that.

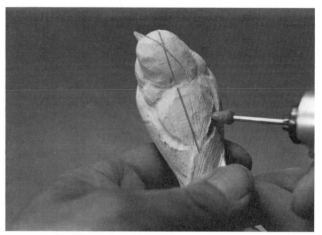

Work on the cape. Make a depression ⅛ inch deep where the cape should be. Here, too, some imagination must be exercised. Making the groove is best done when the Foredom tool is running at a high speed.

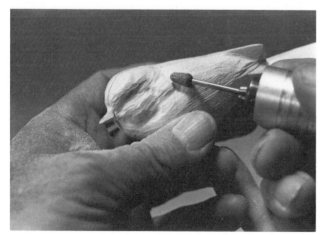

These little valleys are blended toward the rear of the bird and then toward the front of the bird. The bumps can be retained with no sharp edges.

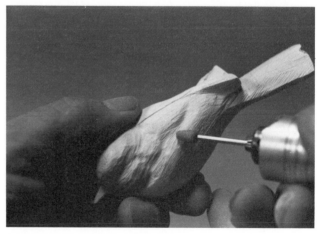

The valleys or grooves are smoothed out by rounding them in each direction.

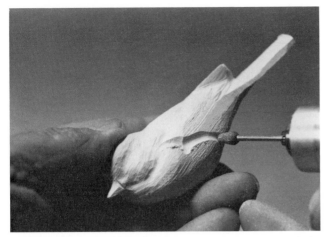

The side pockets are defined. They can be penciled in or drawn with the running Foredom.

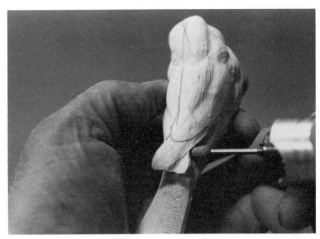

The ruby carver can undercut the bottom edge of the primaries. Work the bit in slightly underneath the left-hand wing.

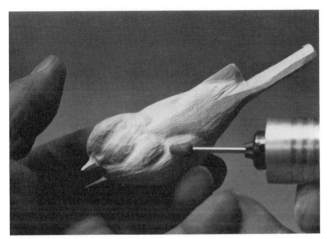

Smooth out the side pockets from the deepest part of the valley to the back of the bird. This leaves more of a gradual curve than from the valley toward the front, which has a more severe transition.

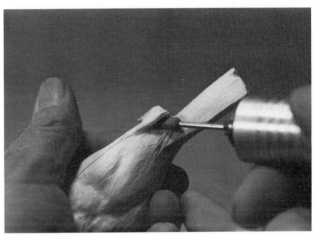

Since the right wing is lapped over the left wing, the bottom edge is undercut and relieved. Later a pointed ruby carver can finish the under-cutting.

Draw the outline of the upper wing.

With the same ruby carver, muscles are outlined on the chest, belly, and rump. Note the crevice down the center of the chest.

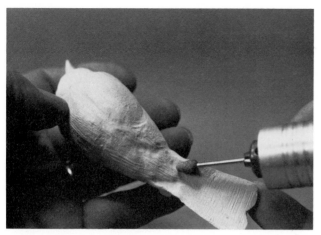

Smooth out the sharp valleys and blend everything together. Thin the tail down a little.

Locate the eyes. If the pencil were to draw a line straight down from where its point is, and the beak were brought in to where it should go, the line would meet the beginning of the beak separation.

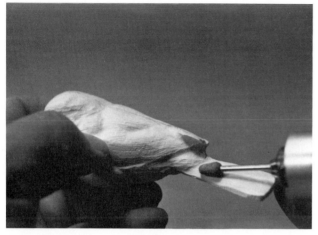

Finish defining the top of the tail, leaving a transition where the tail meets the rump. Also, the tail has to be curved slightly by carving away the planes on either side of the tail's centerline.

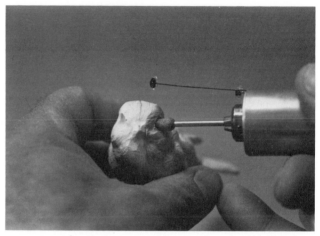

Look at the bird head on, making sure that one eye is not higher than the other. Then look straight down at the top of the head. The eye holes are gouged out with that same pear-shaped ruby carver. Keep checking that one eye is not higher than the other as wood is removed. The clip on the Foredom handpiece holds the 6-millimeter brown eye needed.

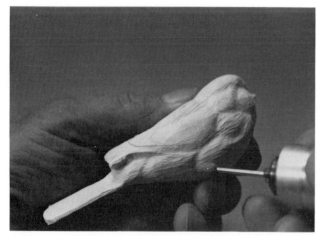

This is what Ernie calls fine-tuning all the crevices and valleys on the bird.

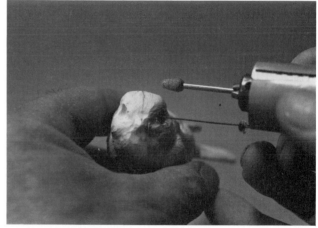

With the glass eye close to the work, it can be used to check the size and depth of the hole without putting the grinding tool down. The outside of the eyes should be flush with the outside of the bird.

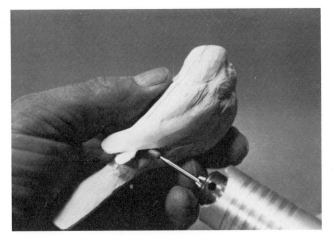

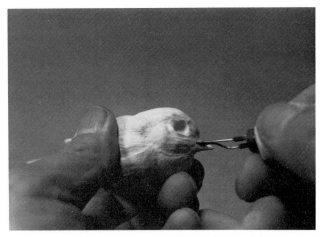

Undercut the wings with a number 19 pointed ruby carver. The wings have been sanded with 150-grit sandpaper so that the wood can take pencil lines. If tupelo is used, it sands with little trouble.

With the burning pen still in hand, burn the separation of the upper and lower bill.

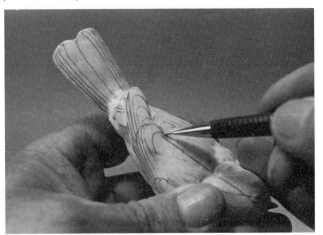

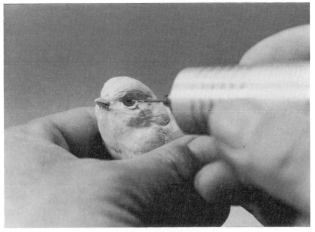

Draw in the feather groupings.

Drill a hole for the eye wire in each hole. With some luck, the drill holes will meet somewhere in the middle, indicating that the eyes are probably symmetrical. Leaving the wires attached makes it easier to handle the eyes, and it helps position them so that they are not canted one way or the other.

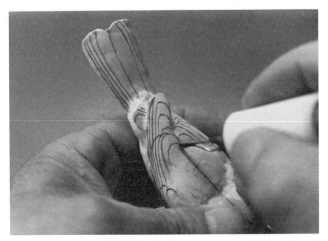

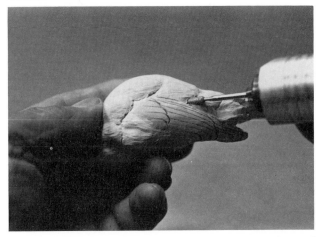

A tight round burning pen on a low heat setting scores around each feather. This makes it possible to go back and separate them slightly. If just pencil lines were left at this time, they would disappear with handling. The burning groove is permanent. Do the same for the tail feathers. The feathers could be stepped down at this stage, using a number 18 ruby carver the head of which has been flattened.

The same pointed ruby carver undercuts the side pocket feathers and feather groupings so they look as if they are overlapping from the front to the back.

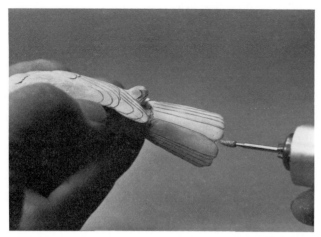

With the same ruby carver, remove wood between the feathers of the tail and outline its edges.

A piece of 280-grit sandpaper wrapped around a mandible does some smoothing of the bird.

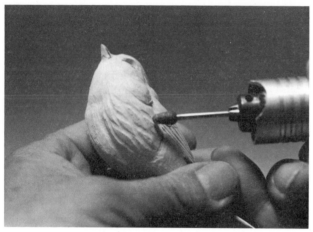

Here the chest can be made more interesting. On a skin, these feathers are more like hairs. A number 23 ruby carver does the job.

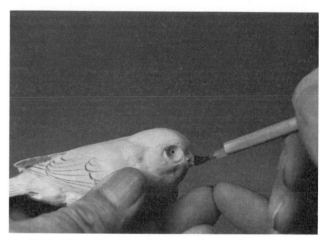

Brush Krazy Glue on the bill to harden it. Be careful not to get any on the rest of the bird. When Krazy Glue is burned, it causes toxic fumes. Do it an hour before the eyes are set in. It also seals the bill so that the water used for putting the eyes in won't get on the bill and distort or swell it.

Smoothing the valleys or grooves out makes everything blend together. Work from the back to the front, dragging the tool.

The bird has had its eye set in with Elmer's Glue and the gap filled with a two-part epoxy. A pointy brush and water can shape the lids. The legs, made of 16-gauge wire, have also been put into the bird. Their scales can be made with a diamond bit. The upper parts of the legs or thighs are made of Tuf Carv, a woodlike epoxy. Tuf Carv can be shaped with a ruby carver.

Sanding should be done wherever water got on the bird when the eyelids were shaped.

The chest and flanks are also burned with lines, not feathers. This, too, is done with a tight round at a low setting. It should be just hot enough so that it leaves a dent in the wood. Check to see if the pen is sinking into the wood without leaving a brown or dark mark. If the wood is scorched, go over the area with gesso to fill up the burns.

Draw in the areas on the chin and head called the bib and cap. Burning is done with a medium setting and a sharp-pointed burning tip. These areas are more like hair than feathers, so just lines are burned in, but some should be curving in, some curving out.

The back is burned very lightly. There are no definite feathers but instead groups of hairs that form blended strands.

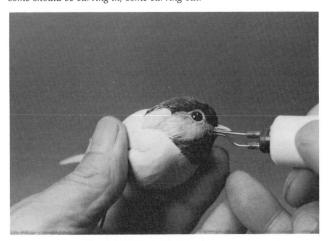

Burn in the cheeks. The feathers radiate out and sweep toward the back. These are burned with a tight round point at a zero setting.

The back, the chest, and the cheeks are done. The wings are burned lightly.

The upper part of the tail is burned with a tight round at a very low setting. Fancy burning is not required for a chickadee.

Using a mixture of gesso and water, about half and half, apply one coat on all areas not burned dark. One more coat is put on the tail, and three more coats are put on the chest and rump. Check that the coats are making the bird progressively lighter.

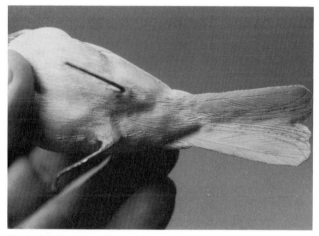

The underside of the tail. Note that no feathers are separated or relieved. Individual rows of feathers don't have to be burned. One stroke can go across the tail. The Tuf Carv that formed the thighs can be burned if the pen is at a low setting.

Apply the second, third, and fourth coats to the chest area.

Seal the bird with 1301 Krylon acrylic spray. A straight lacquer thinned with lacquer thinner is preferable on larger birds with a variety of burning lines. If 1301 is used, spray the bird until the excess drips off, and leave it to dry at least six to eight hours before painting it.

The chickadee is ready to be given its acrylic colors.

Paint with a mixture of burnt umber and ultramarine blue. Each is mixed separately as washes, then mixed until a gray is achieved that matches the gray on the study skin or picture references. Test it on a piece of white paper. Leave the outside edges of the wing and tail feathers light.

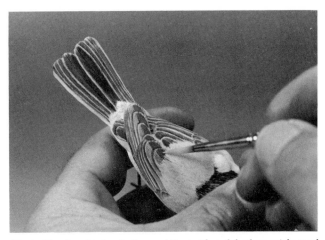

The inside of each wing feather and the inside tail feathers might need five or six washes to darken them. This varies the tones to make the overall bird more interesting.

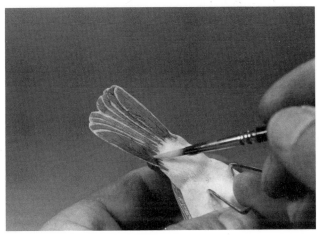

Do the same on the underside of the tail.

Put a wash over the whole wing and tail area with ultramarine and burnt umber. It blends everything together. The back might take three to four coats of that wash. If it comes up too brown, put a light blue wash on it. If it looks too gray, go back over it with some brown wash. This is a procedure that takes time and effort, Ernie cautions.

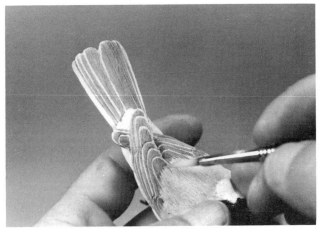

Put a second coat on the top of the bird. This may have to be done two or three times to get the right shade.

The top of the bird is finished.

Some of the dark areas may need more darkening. Where areas overlap, false shadows can be put in with more washes.

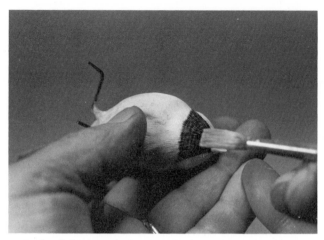

Feather flicking can also break up the dark color on the bib area.

Wash the flanks with raw umber, burnt sienna, and yellow ochre until a buffy yellowish brown is attained.

The outer edges of the feathers are touched up with white and a long, thin brush. These are the secondary feathers being outlined. Do the same for the edge of the tail.

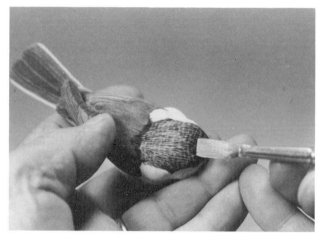

A sable brush that has been trimmed is loaded with a mix of white paint and water. Just touching the edge to the bird leaves a small line of white. This feather flicking breaks up the top, dark color.

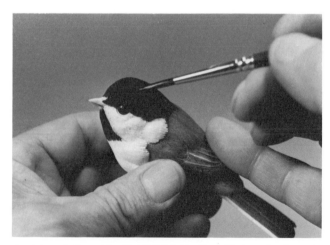

A mixture of ultramarine blue and burnt umber will give a deep brown to touch up the color of the head and chin. The white feather flicking will show up as a hint of feathers.

A knife blade can clean up any paint left around or on the glass eyes.

The bird is set up on its branch. Note the cast pewter and lead toes added with just glue.

The back of a finished chickadee.

The same chickadee can be adapted to a simple piece of wood flattened on its bottom.

Immature Black-capped Chickadee

Black-capped Chickadee

Black-capped Chickadee

130

Immature White-throated Sparrow

Immature Bluebirds

Immature Bluebirds

Carolina Wren

Meadowlark

Meadowlark

Meadowlark

Robin

Robin

Robin

Robin

Downy Woodpecker

Downy Woodpecker

Downy Woodpecker

Downy Woodpecker

Evening Grosbeak

144

Evening Grosbeak

Cardinal

146

Cardinal

Cardinal

148

Cardinal

Bluejay Family

Bluejay Family

Bluejay Family

Bluejay Family

Bluejay Family

Immature Cardinal

Immature Cardinal

Immature Wood Thrush

Immature Wood Thrush

Immature Wood Thrush

White-throated Sparrow

White-throated Sparrow

Immature Titmouse

Long-tailed Titmouse

Immature White-throated Sparrow

Immature White-throated Sparrow

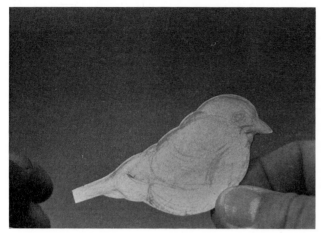

The side profile pattern of a baby white-throated sparrow.

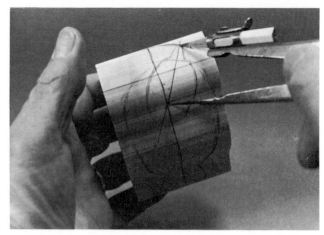

Establish a turned head by putting a compass on the highest part of the head and swinging the compass around to the right. Redraw the head with a new centerline.

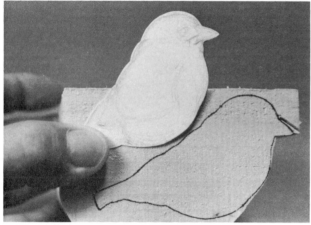

Transfer the pattern to a piece of tupelo, favoring the grain with the run of the bill and the direction of the tail. These are areas that need strength.

Begin cutting away wood, starting at either side of the beak and the tail.

Cut as close as possible to the outline of the bird.

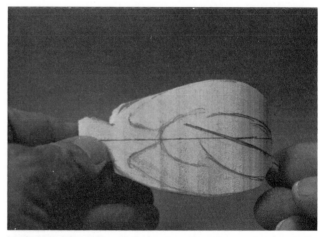

Work around the profile with the bandsaw. Removing wood as done in the previous step allows the blade to make a clean sweep around the outline. Note the centerlines that will remain throughout most of the rough carving.

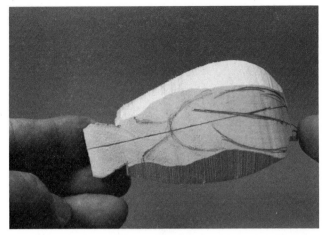

Round the edges off with the bandsaw. Care must be taken doing this. Since the bird is not resting flush on the bandsaw table, the blade will have a tendency to bind and pull the piece away.

Put the cheek in and establish the Muehlmatt bump. A real bird is compared for bill size and its relationship to the eyes. (Ernie says a study skin does not offer very much else.)

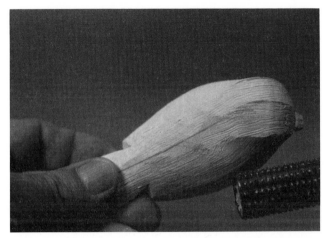

With a ¾-inch-diameter Arco rotary rasp, roughly shape the bird. Don't forget to leave the centerline intact.

Once satisfied with the shape of the head, go on to the back and define where the secondary feathers will be, which will be recessed slightly. This is done with the same pear-shaped ruby carver.

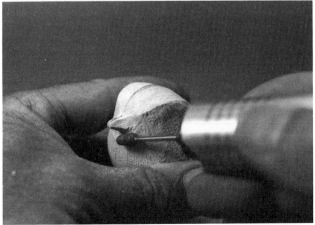

With a number 23 pear-shaped ruby carver, clean up the bill, establishing the two top and three bottom planes. Like the body, the bill should have a centerline for reference.

The results of the feather defining can be studied here.

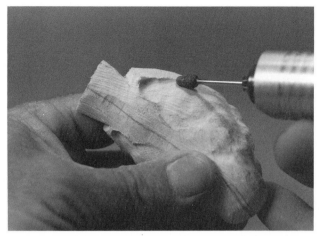

Since the wings are recessed into the bird, more recessing must be done with the ruby carver. Make sure the rump sticks up above the wings.

Make depressions with the pear-shaped ruby carver for the eyes.

Blend all valleys and grooves into the body with the ruby carver. Also, work the wood so that the chest feathers appear to be overlapping the wings slightly.

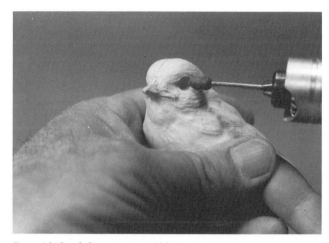

For a right-handed person, it would be best to do the bird's right eye first. Then the bird can be looked at face to face, and the left eye hole can be made. This makes it possible to see how level the eyes are without changing the Foredom from one hand to the other or wrapping the hand around the bird's head. Don't forget to drill small holes for the glass eye wires.

Draw the eyes in and the fleshy part of the beak. Notice how the beak's origin is almost in line with the leading edge of the eye.

Separate the upper and lower beak with a burning pen and a tight round tip.

After sanding the sides, draw in the primary and secondary feathers and the feathers for the tail.

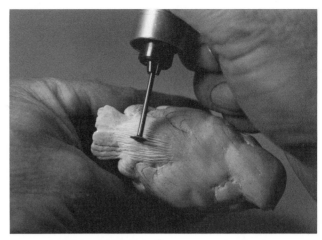

With a grinding stone, make some grooves on the rump to give the impression of hair, or what Ernie calls a shaggy appearance. These will later be burned over.

Outline the feathers with the burning pen.

Here the bird, with thighs made of Tuf Carv and 16-gauge wire added for legs, can be studied. Also, the bill has been hardened with Krazy Glue. It is ready for burning.

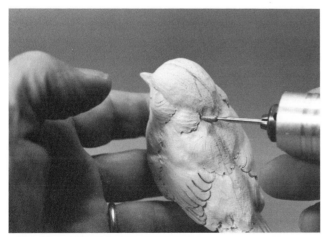

With a number 19 ruby carver, do some detail work around the cheeks and where the chest feathers lap over on the body to further exaggerate them. Undercut them slightly.

The eyes should be put in place before burning. This baby sparrow takes 6-millimeter brown eyes that are set in with Elmer's Glue. The lids are made of a two-part plumber's expoxy that can be moved and shaped with a pointed brush and water.

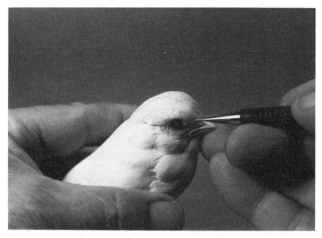

Draw small feathers on either side of what will be dark stripes and between them on the head.

When the cheeks and sides of the face are burned, draw in the feathers of the two dark stripes.

With the tight round tip and a low heat setting, burn these feathers that will later be painted white by making lines to fit within each semicircular feather.

With a pointed burning tip, make the pen hot enough to leave dark marks. Note how the feathers are staggered and are of different sizes. Also burn in the little eye stripes that run from either side of the eyes to the back of the head and to the top of the beak.

Draw in the cheek feathers.

Draw in feathers on the chest. Make them different sizes and stagger them.

Burn in the chest feathers lightly with the tight round.

The feathers on the sides are burned lightly.

The burn lines on the chest can be studied.

The feathers on the back are also burned with a low heat setting.

Draw in the feathers on the back. These are basically in line and staggered only slightly.

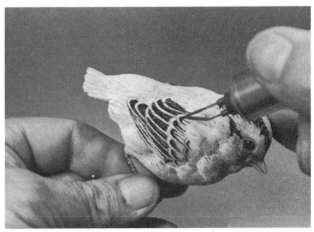

Burn in the dark areas on the wing coverts, the secondaries, and the primaries, leaving a light edge on each feather.

Burn the center parts of the back feathers darker than the outer edges. Make them a deep brown to imitate the color of the feather patterns as they naturally appear on the bird.

Apply watered-down gesso to all the light areas: the edges of the feathers, the tail, the rump, the wing edges, and the wing bars on the coverts.

Make some dark streaks on the rump and tail feathers.

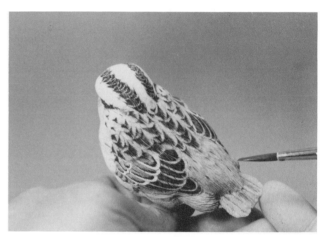

With a mix of burnt umber, ultramarine blue, and a warm black, paint in the brown areas.

Burn in some dark streaks on the chest and some dark dots around the eyes. Also outline a bib under the beak with dark burn lines. This area will later be painted white.

A darker mix with more warm black in it is applied to the centers of the back feathers, the upper parts of the secondary feathers, the major part of the primary feathers, and the two stripes on top of the head.

There is little else to paint on the bird. The rump may need one or two more washes of the brown mix to darken it. The gray takes more of a grayish brown with light edges.

The white bib is gesso with a wash of burnt umber to take the starkness out of the white. The chest is a gray, gotten by mixing ultramarine blue and burnt umber. Right underneath the bib may have six coats of gray, ¼ inch down only five coats, and so on to make the gray progressively lighter. The beak is washed with a matte medium and a gray, which is also a mix of burnt umber and ultramarine blue. Make the tip darker than the rest. This may require ten washes. The fleshy parts of the beak are left almost wood-colored.

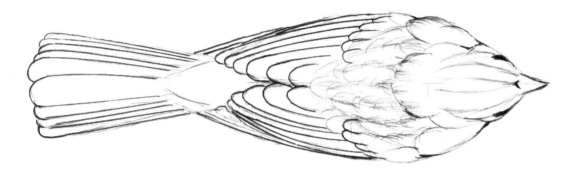

White-throated Sparrow

Immature Bluebird

Immature Bluebird

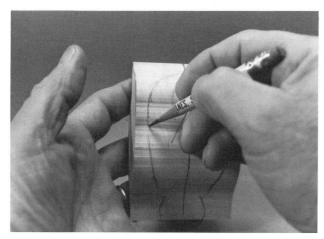

The side profile has already been cut, and the top profile must be drawn. Ernie says it's done really by eye, using what he calls a vivid imagination.

A ¾-inch-diameter rotary rasp can be used to cut wood away on either side of the head and get it down to its correct width.

After the top profile is cut, round off the edges with a bandsaw blade.

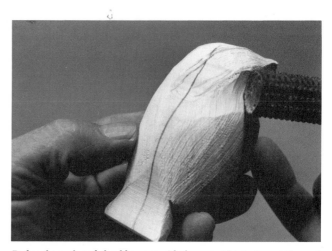

Define the neck and shoulder area with the rasp. This is done at the neck area.

Here is the top profile with the head turned, which is done with a compass rotated from the highest point on the head.

Establish the width of the eyes, which is about ¾ inch. It is something you have to visualize while looking at the bird head on. If the eye channels look too close together, Ernie suggests discarding the wood and starting over.

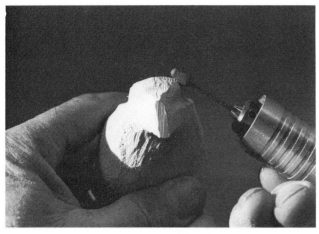

Round off the top of the head with a number 23 pear-shaped ruby carver.

Draw in the cape with the ruby carver, making a valley and blending it into the rest of the body.

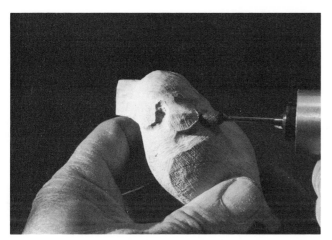

Carve in the cheeks and the bumps behind the cheeks, the Muehlmatt bumps, with the same ruby carver.

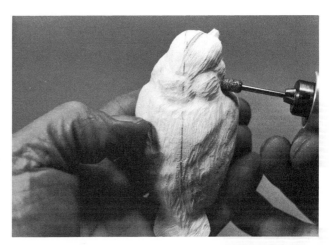

Work on the shoulder area, undercutting slightly.

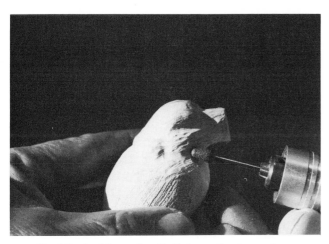

Blend the cheek bumps into the bird, rounding the wood over.

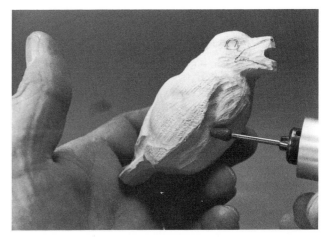

Muscle detail can be put on the chest. Also at this time, draw in the eye locations and the open bill. Note how the origin of the bill lies directly under the front edge of the eye.

Take the ruby carver and remove the wood between the mandibles or jaws.

This is what Ernie calls fine-tuning the bird, going over it to define or redefine muscles and bumps. Here an area is carved away where the tail meets the rump.

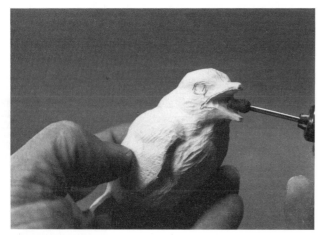

Most of the wood is removed.

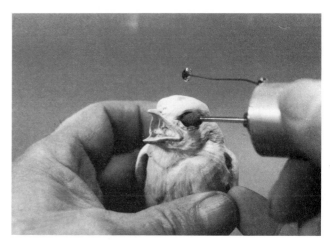

Drill out the eye holes with the same ruby carver.

A small ball-shaped diamond cutter and a high-speed grinding tool can put in the mouth detail and tongue.

Check the eye openings with the glass eyes put in in reverse.

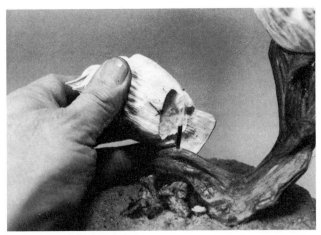

If the bird is to be fitted to a branch, the underside of the rump has to be hollowed slightly. A piece of carbon paper placed between the wood and the bird will leave dark marks. This will indicate where to start grinding wood away on the bird. Also note the pin that holds the bird on the branch.

Go around each feather with a tight round tip and burning pen. They can also be layered with a flattened, barrel-shaped, number 18 ruby carver.

This is a composition with two baby bluebirds.

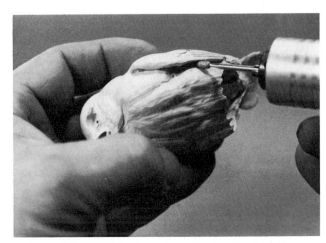

With a number 19 ruby carver, undercut the wings, leaving a slight gap.

The wing area should be sanded lightly and the wing feathers drawn in pencil. Ernie says there is little differentiation between the secondaries and primaries on a baby bird. Also, the feathers are not very orderly.

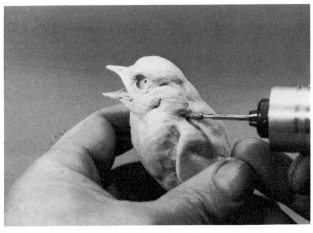

Undercutting can also be done on the cheeks, under the Muehlmatt bumps, and where the bill meets the head.

With a high-speed grinding tool and a diamond bit, undercut the wing feathers and the cheeks.

Brushing the bird with just water will raise the grain before the next step. Let it dry overnight.

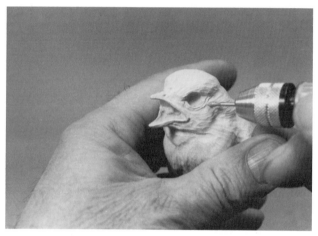

Do the same around the eyes.

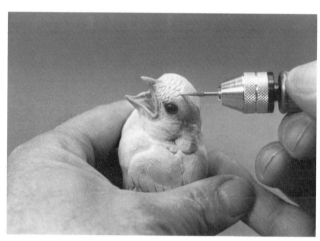

Use a needle-pointed diamond cutter and the high-speed grinder to outline the small feathers on the forehead.

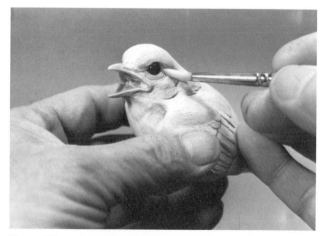

The 6-millimeter brown eyes have been put in place with Elmer's Glue and covered with a two-part epoxy, which can be shaped with a pointed brush and water.

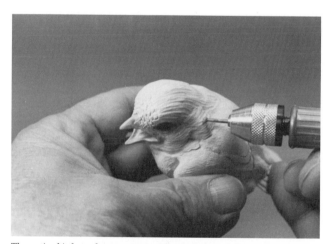

The entire bird can be gone over with a ball-shaped diamond bit, only ⅛ inch in diameter. Done in place of sanding with paper, the many small grooves will also vary the surface and create a soft look when it is burned and painted.

When using the bit, work in the direction of the feather flow.

Use a fiber brush to go over the bird and remove any fuzz or burrs left.

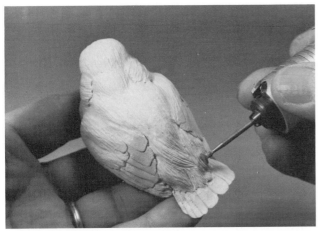

Grind some feathers in the rump with a grinding stone. Ernie calls this area shaggy.

This is the first step in the burning. Draw feathers on the cheek.

Finish the "sanding" on the wings, working in the direction of the barb lines.

With a tight round tip, burn lines around the eyes, having the lines flowing toward the back.

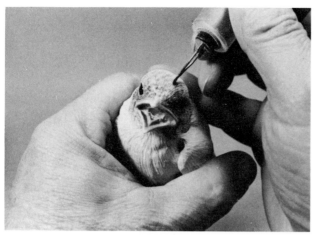

Burn the top of the head lightly with the same tight round tip. There are no dark lines on a baby bluebird.

Work down the back of the bird.

Burn lines on the chest, but burn them in groups, not just straight down. Curve them to meet each other, following the grooves in the bird.

Make the feathers on the upper part of the wings.

Curve the lines to meet each other and follow the grooves put in with the small ball-shaped diamond bit.

Note the flow of burn lines on these wing feathers.

Burn lines on the rump over the stoning grooves and the rump, all with a low heat setting.

White streaks are also found on the upper part of the wings and the back.

Apply a thin coat of one part gesso to three parts water over the entire bird.

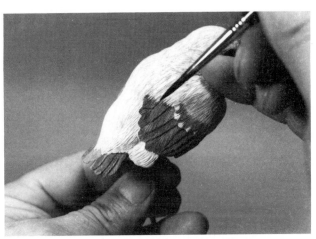

Start by painting the wings with ultramarine blue, burnt umber, and burnt sienna. The wings are split with color. Bright blue shows on the lower halves of the feathers below the quill lines and dark blue on the upper halves above the quill lines.

The chest of a baby bluebird is streaked with white. Apply four coats of the thinned-down gesso on it. The surrounding areas are darker.

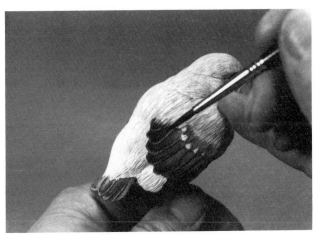

Leave the edges of the feathers light.

The painting so far can be studied here.

The bill is washed with yellow ochre on the lips and burnt sienna, ultramarine blue, and matte medium. The mix is one part matte medium, one part water, and a brushful of the paint for the upper part of the beak. Do that about ten times until a waxy, boney look is achieved.

A gray for the back and chest is made of a mix of ultramarine blue and burnt sienna. Paint around and through each light mark. Ernie says it takes about six passes, staggering each one so that one or two might cross the white marks while others go around them. This makes for a fuzzy appearance. Also do some feather flicking with white on the rump area with a trimmed brush. The tail is a dark mix of ultramarine blue and burnt sienna, as is the head. Do the head with six to seven washes.

The inside of the mouth is done in a pale, reddish orange. This is a signal for the mother returning with food. Note the streaks on the chest.

The underside of the tail is done with a blue-gray wash.

Three birds make up this composition.

A closeup shows their details.

Another closeup shows their back details.

Carolina Wren

Carolina Wren

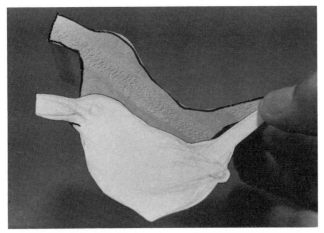

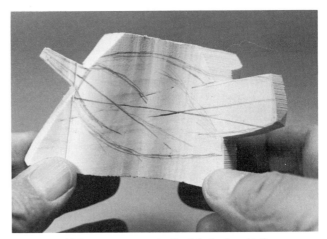

The Carolina wren pattern is an original one based on, but not copied exactly from, a photo of a wren. The tail will be cocked to one side and the wings will be crossed. Ernie calls this an interesting position.

Make stop cuts on each side of the beak and tail.

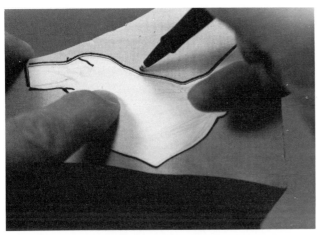

The pattern is traced onto the wood with a marking pencil.

From the stop cuts, make a continuous arc with the bandsaw blade to remove the rest of the excess wood.

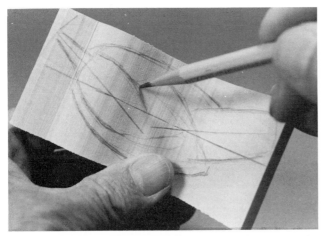

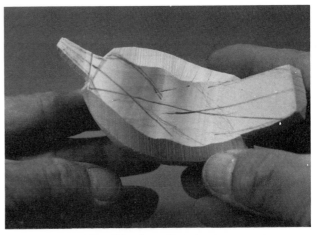

The side profile is cut out and the top is drawn. Put the compass point where the neck will be turning from underneath the head. This should put it at the highest spot on the head. Draw the new beak and forehead and a new centerline. Do the same for the tail. Some knowledge of bird anatomy would help here, Ernie says, as well as a study skin.

Take off the edges with the bandsaw.

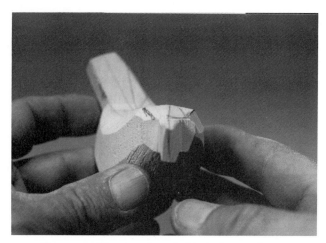

Draw a pencil line down the end of the beak as a reference.

Using the same carbide cutter, round the bandsawed edges on the chest, the back, and the tail.

The dark lines on the wren's head indicate where some shaping has to be done to round it off. Also, round off the top of the breast area slightly with a cutter.

Since the wings will be crossed, right wing over left wing, establish the bottom edge of the top wing with a pencil line.

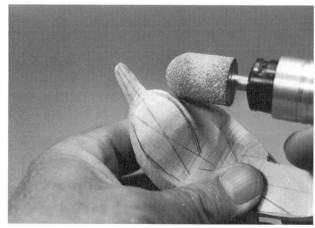

A carbide cutter with a rounded end can roughly shape the head and establish its width. As to how wide it should be, Ernie says the only way you can know for sure is to capture a Carolina wren and make the bird stand still. With a study skin, most of the skull may have been removed, making the skin useless for measurements.

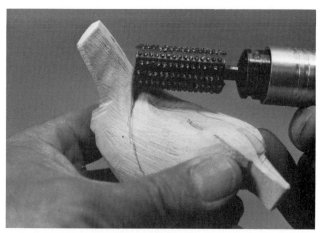

Use a cutter with a sharp edge and cut down on that line to establish a flat edge. This requires cutting down into the body.

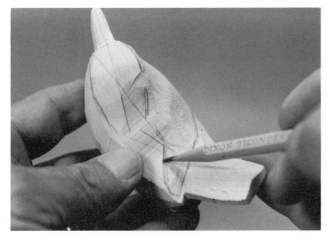

With a pencil, establish the width of that upper wing.

If the layout of the wings looks satisfactory, go to the head and work on the beak. Draw a centerline on the top of the beak.

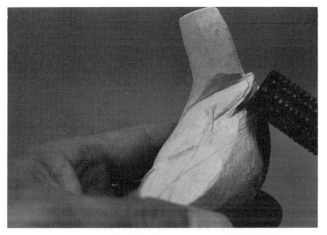

Undercut the right wing that sticks up on the left side of the body.

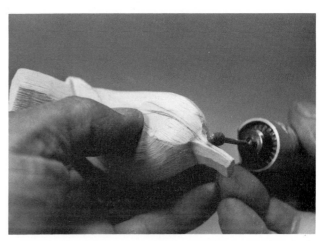

Establish the five planes of the beak with the number 23 pear-shaped ruby carver.

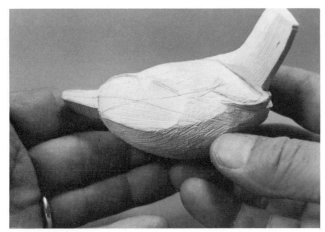

Here can be studied the wren so far. Ernie says he worked on the wings before the head to make sure he could have the feathers overlap properly. He also suggests that this may be an ambitious project for a beginner because of the tail being cocked to the right of the crossed primaries.

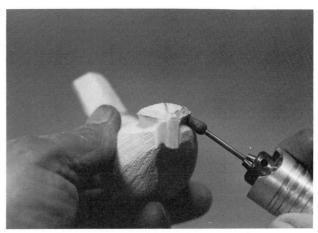

With the same ruby carver, make the channels for the eyes and round over any sharp edges left above and below those channels.

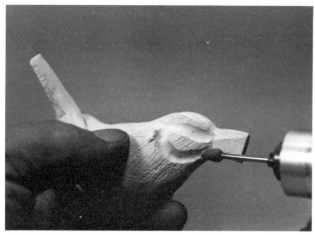

Make the cheeks of the bird. Don't forget the Muehlmatt bumps behind the cheeks.

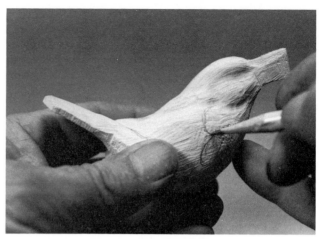

Pencil in where the chest will go. This will have a scalloped look on either side.

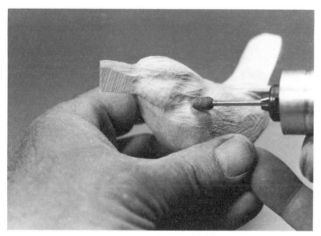

Blend the body and the cheeks together with the ruby carver.

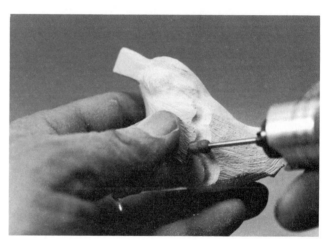

The chest is defined with the ruby carver and extends to the flank.

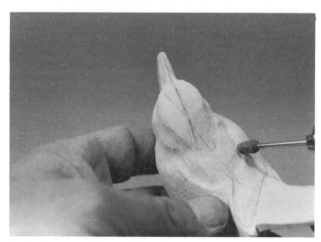

Define the cape, which extends back to meet the secondary feathers of the wings.

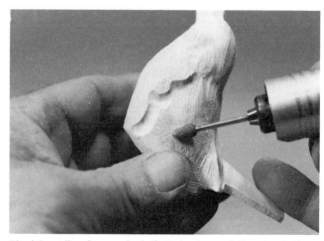

Blend the scalloped grooves back, flattening the wood. Note that the fronts of the grooves will have more of a curvature than the edges in the rear.

In the middle of the bird's sides are what Ernie describes as wing muscles. Those, too, get blended toward the rear of the bird. Also do some undercutting on the crossed primaries.

Work on the rump, removing wood on the underside of the tail, and put in grooves to represent clumps of rump feathers.

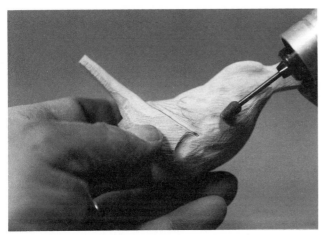

Blend the wing muscle grooves or depressions with the rest of the body.

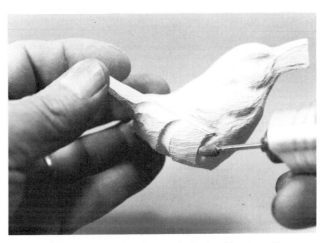

Note how far the grooves extend up on the flanks. After these clumps are defined, blend them into the body. Ernie says it does not matter whether they can actually be found on the bird; what matters is that they break up an otherwise continuous plane of wood.

Pencil in the wing feathers.

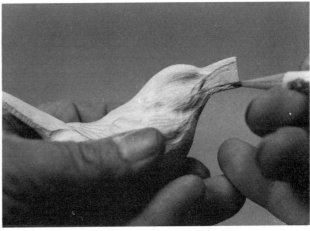

Draw in the separation of the upper and lower beak. Make sure it goes far enough back into the head so that it lies underneath the fronts of the eyes.

Remove wood between the two mandibles or jaws.

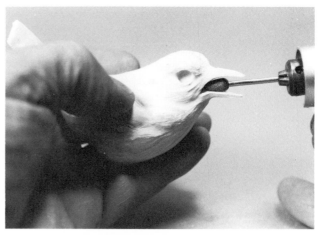

Hollow out the inside of the mouth as much as possible.

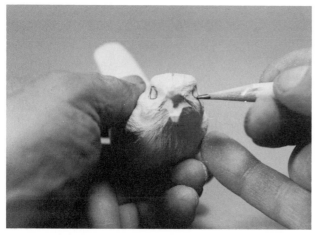

A right-handed person should draw in the bird's right eye first, then its left eye, so that the bird can be looked at head on to make sure the eyes are level. Look at it from above to see that one eye is not too far forward or back.

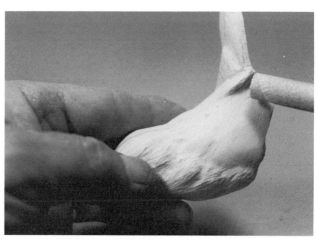

Use a sanding roll on the rump and wings. This can be just a piece of sandpaper held in a split shaft called a mandrel. A rubber band will keep the paper from unrolling.

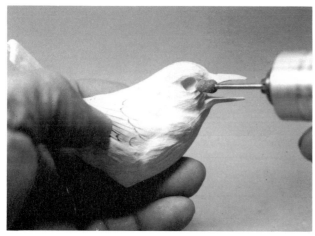

Make the eye holes for 6-millimeter brown eyes.

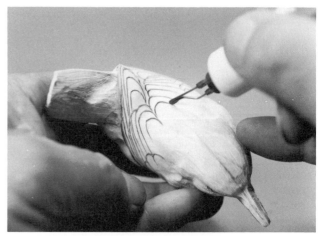

Burn around each of the feathers on the two wings.

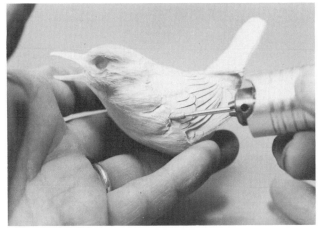

With a number 19 pointed ruby carver, undercut some of the chest feathers where they overlap the body.

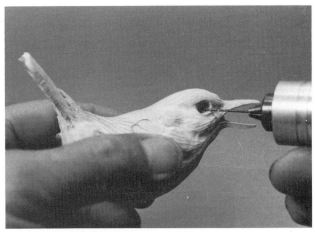

Drill the centerholes for the eye wires. A tiny drill in a Foredom will do the job.

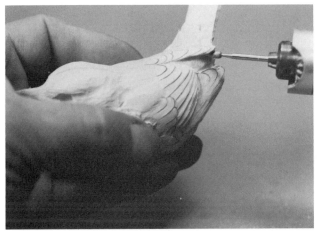

Undercut with the same ruby carver where the one wing overlaps the rump. Leave the wing as thin as possible at its end.

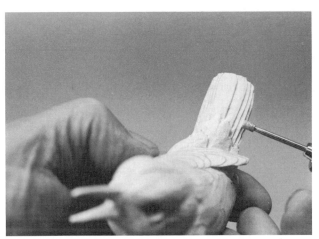

With a barrel-shaped, number 18 ruby carver, which has its end ground flat, step down the feathers on the tail.

Still with the pointed ruby carver, shape the inside of the mouth.

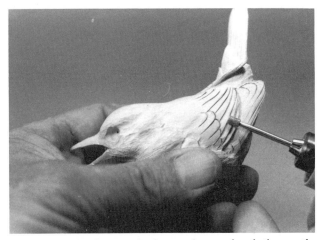

The same stepping down can be done on the secondary feathers on the wings.

With the number 19 ruby carver, the nostrils and separation between the head and bill can be defined.

Finish sanding the bird.

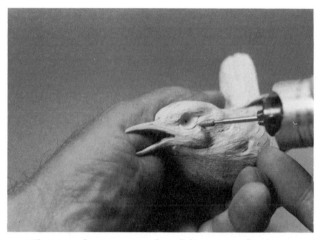

The same ruby carver can make a slight ring around each eye.

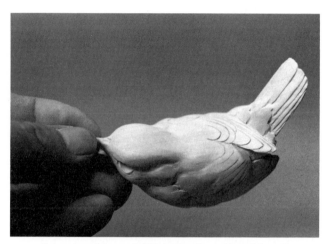

A top view of the sanded bird. Note the position of the tail.

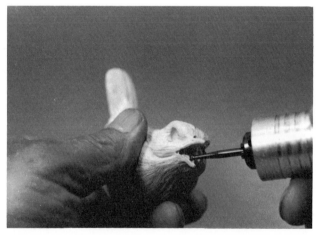

A ball-shaped diamond bit can put a tongue and more of a throat in the mouth.

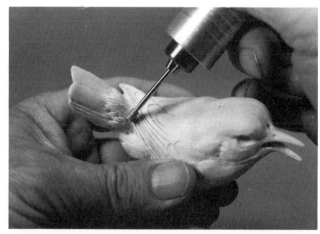

A diamond wheel or this barrel-shaped ruby carver can put in some groups of hairy feathers on the rump.

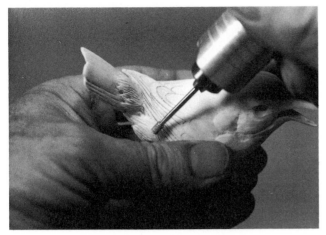

Do the same on the flanks of the bird.

The bird is fitted to its base.

Apply Krazy Glue to the bill. This will keep it from breaking should it be bumped. Put at least two coats on it because glue readily soaks into the wood.

The eyes can be put into place and the Tuf Carv thighs stoned, though they could be burned at a low setting.

A side view of the bird shows the legs in place and the Tuf Carv thighs. Shaping the filler is not necessary because it will be detailed later. A diamond cutter cuts in the scales on the legs.

The stoning is finished, and putty should have been put around the eyes and shaped with a brush and water.

After drawing ⅛-inch-long feathers on the head, burn with a tight round at a low setting.

This bird has white stripes above the eyes and a dark area that projects from the rear of the eyes toward the back. Burn some medium brown marks to outline these stripes. This might be a 2 or 3 setting on a burning tool.

Draw feathers on the cheeks and on the Muehlmatt bump.

Burn the chest with a low heat setting.

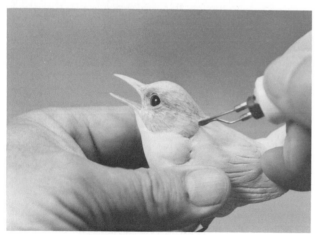

Burn these feathers with the tight round tip at a low heat setting.

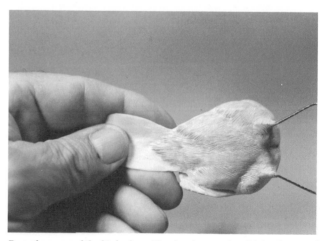

Burn the rump of the bird, also with a low heat setting. Make clusters of feathers instead of a lot of parallel lines.

Burn the back of the bird and the rump. The back has lines that suggest hair rather than individual feathers. Try to blend them into each other.

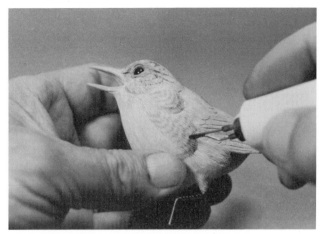

With a slightly higher heat than has been used for most of the burning, perhaps a 1 setting, burn some shades that suggest vermiculation. This setting is open to experimentation, says Ernie. Also governing the amount of heat coming through to the wood is the amount of metal in the tip. A tip that has been sharpened will get hotter than one that has not been put to a stone.

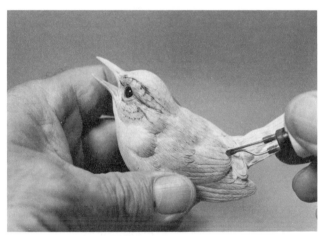

Burn the wings at a low heat setting.

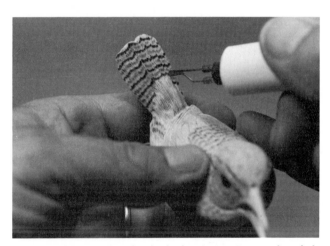

Burn the dark bars on the tail with a hot burning pen. Between those dark bars, burn medium brown lines.

Burn the bottom of the tail. Note that continuous lines can be made from the quills and across the underlapping feathers.

Burn the dark bars on the wings and the tiny bars on the wing coverts. Do the same on the back, but do not burn between them.

The rump feathers have black Vs in them. Also do the black bars on the underside of the tail. (It does not have the two-tone color the top of the tail has.)

The thinned-down gesso is applied between each of the black bars on the primaries.

The bird is ready to be painted and primed with Krylon 1301 or lacquer diluted with lacquer thinner.

A wash of raw umber, which can be toned down with a bit of ultramarine blue, is applied over the wings, not the primaries, as well as the back and tail.

The white eye stripes and the chest are painted with thinned-down gesso.

Note what has been painted with the raw umber wash. The chest, however, is a mix of yellow ochre and raw umber. Ernie describes it as a buffy color.

The bird is fully painted with the beak coated with one part matte medium, one part water, and a touch of warm black. Give the beak about ten washes of this mix, but leave the edges lighter than the middle.

The bird is placed on its perch. Cast feet are in place.

Meadowlark

Meadowlark

Adult Meadowlark

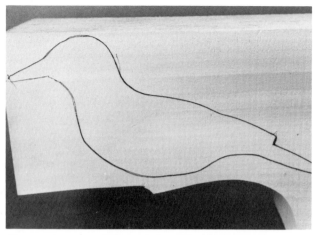

Choose a piece of wood about 3 inches wide, with the grain favoring the beak and the tail. Ernie describes the meadowlark as a husky bird that requires a thick block to work with.

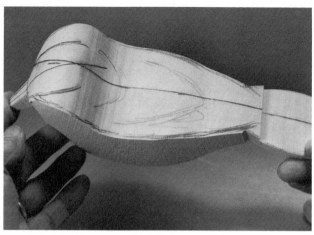

Cut the rest of the top profile, making an arc from the tail to the head.

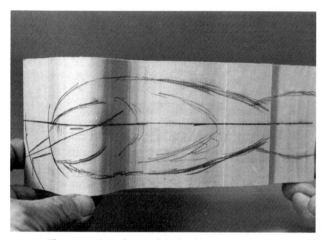

The pattern is in place and the head is turned to its left.

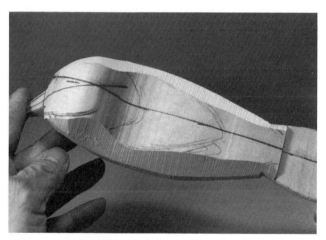

Round off the sharp corners with the bandsaw.

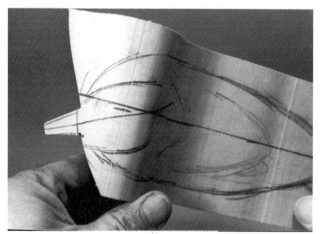

Cut in on either side of the beak and remove the wood. Do the same on the tail.

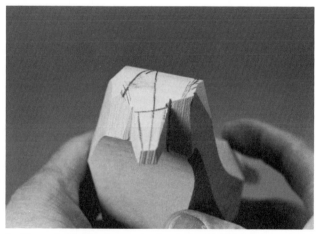

Looking at the bird head on, notice that the head is high-looking to the left of the centerline. The head has to be rounded over without removing too much wood. Work from the centerline right, and then take off part of the left side that is too high. Note the line drawn on the left.

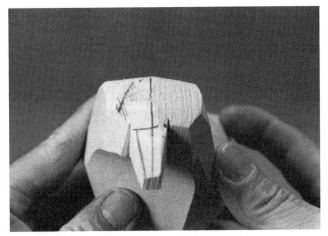

The wood can be removed with a carbide cutter.

With the same tool, remove wood at the neck.

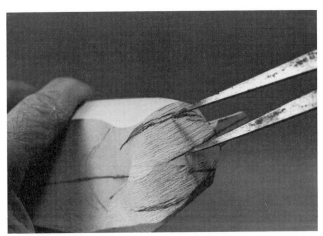

Check with calipers that the head is the right width. Ernie says the width at this point, probably at the top of the eye channels, is 1⅛ inches. The width at the cheeks should be about 1⅜ inches.

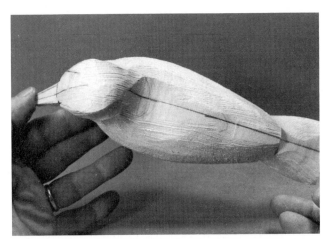

Round the body with the rotary rasp. At the fattest part of the body, the cross section should be a circle. Leave the centerline in place.

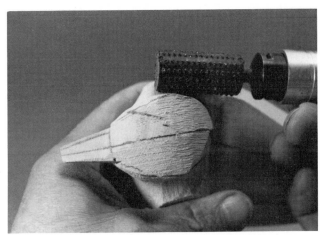

Round off the head with a rotary rasp or a large carbide cutter.

Check that the head is symmetrical and that the proper curvature is there.

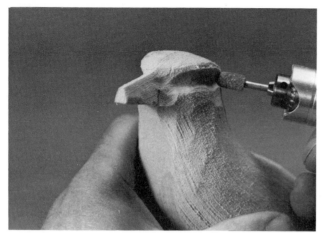

Depress the eye areas with a barrel-shaped carbide cutter. Ernie suggests using this instead of a ruby carver because of the size of the bird.

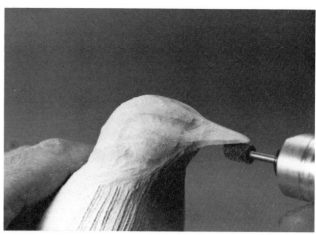

Blend the cheeks and the bumps into the body and define the planes of the beak.

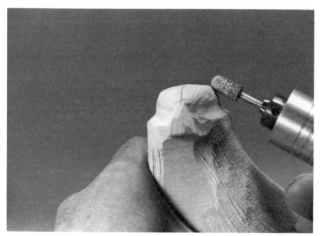

With the same cutter, round over the sharp edges of the depression.

Using a number 23 ruby carver, bring the boundaries of the beak back into the head. Notice the V-shaped area of facial feathers that "arrows" into the beak. Also start to make the lower jaw slightly narrower than the upper one. Then make small depressions in the cheeks.

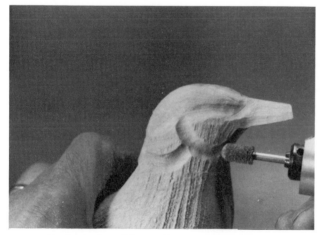

Do the cheeks and the Muehlmatt bumps behind them.

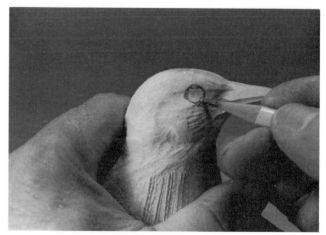

Draw in the circles for 8-millimeter brown eyes.

Take the ruby carver and make the eye holes.

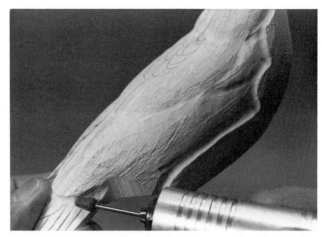

After smoothing the rear edges of the depressions on either side toward the back, define where the wings set down on the rump.

Set the eyes in place with epoxy putty, and use a wet brush to move the epoxy away from the glass. Start in the centers and work out. A small knife blade can make a cut for the corners where the lids meet.

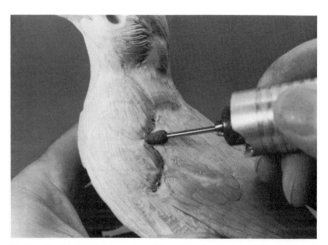

Ernie calls this fine-tuning, a blending of the front edge of the chest and back separation into the body.

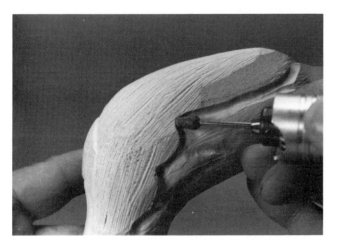

Define the separation of the chest area from the back.

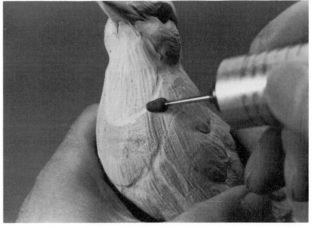

A meadowlark has a black bib on its neck. Where there is an abrupt change of feather color, Ernie will outline the separation by making a slight depression with the ruby carver.

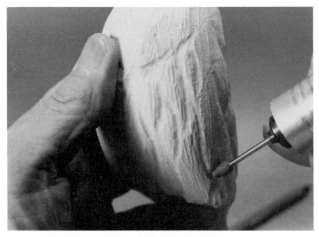

Make some feather groupings on the chest, though the feathers there are more like hair.

Burning can begin on the head. Make lines indicating the two stripes running along the top of the meadowlark's head, and draw in small feathers on the head.

After sanding the wings, pencil in the primary and secondary feathers. Do the same on the tail and outline them with a burning pen.

Burn some of the cheeks with straight lines, though right around the beak individual feathers are visible. This is done with a tight round at a low heat setting.

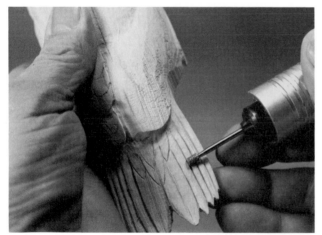

With a flattened number 18 ruby carver, step down the tail feathers. However, it is easier to burn this area if they have not been separated, Ernie says.

The dark stripes are done with a pointed tip with a high setting of 4 or 5 on some burning tools.

Burn some dark marks or wedges on the bumps behind the cheeks and the outer edges on the feathers around the beak. Also burn some long, dark lines on the cheeks.

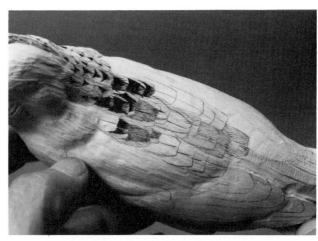

The rest of the back feathers have sea-skate-shaped, dark markings on a medium brown background. Edges are left with the light burn. These feathers, then, require three different burns.

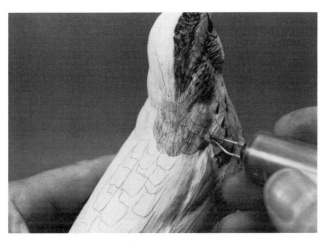

Draw feathers on the back. The meadowlark is unique in that many of the feathers are squared off, looking almost worn away. Burn with the tight round at a light setting.

Draw feathers on the chest, varying their sizes, working the feathers into the bumps where possible. Never draw them across both a high and low area.

On the feathers behind the nape of the head there are arrow-shaped marks. Burn them dark.

Burn the chest feathers lightly.

Put the dark, elongated marks on the chest feathers with the pointed tip.

The wings are burned once lightly, then shaded with a hotter burning pen, leaving the edges light. The dark bars are burned with a hot pen. The bib is also burned darkly.

Outline the secondary and primary feathers with the tight round.

Notice the extent of the dark markings on the chest and down the sides.

Put the barb lines on the wing feathers.

Put the dark markings on the underside of the rump, and burn in the barb lines on the tail feathers, leaving light edges.

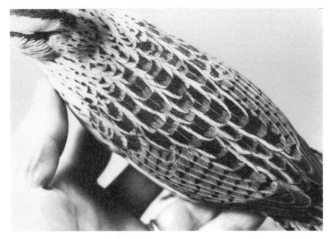

The back of the completely burned meadowlark shows the different shapes of the feathers and the three different burns.

The study skin compared to the wooden bird. Note the squared-off feather edges.

The center feathers on the tail are darker and get lighter toward the outer edges.

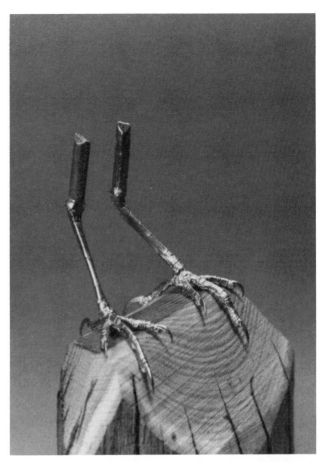

A piece of cedar, representing the top of a post, where a meadowlark might be found, can hold the cast feet for the bird. The legs and toes can be bent to have the bird perch properly.

Holes are drilled on the underside to accept the leg posts. There are no thigh feathers on this bird. The presence of these feathers depends on how the bird is sitting, Ernie says.

The painting is fairly easy, Ernie says. The breast first gets a light coat of gesso. Then one coat of cadmium yellow is applied. Another is applied on the center of the breast, yet not quite to the edges of the wings. Another coat is applied while "withdrawing" the outer boundaries washed with cadmium yellow. This is done about five times so that the yellow fades out from the center of the breast. The primaries and under the tail are given a mix of burnt umber and ultramarine blue. Gesso is applied to any light areas on the back. Washes of raw umber are put on the feather edges while burnt umber is put on the centers of the back feathers.

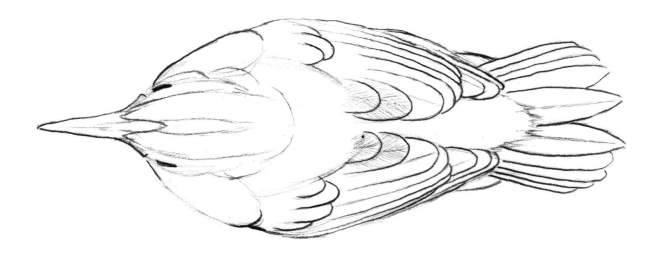

Immature Meadowlark

Robin

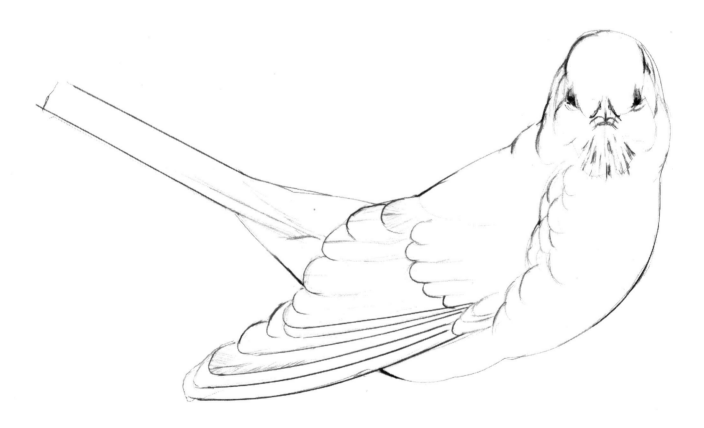

Robin

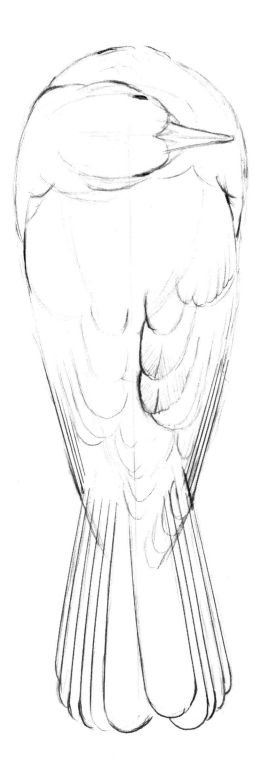

The pattern with some of the details drawn in.

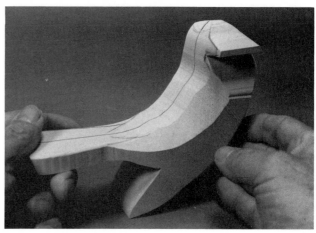

The top profile is drawn to size. Also, the turn of the robin's head at its highest point must be determined.

The side profile cut out on the bandsaw with the centerline drawn. The wood is 3 inches thick, though the bird will actually be only 2½ inches through its center.

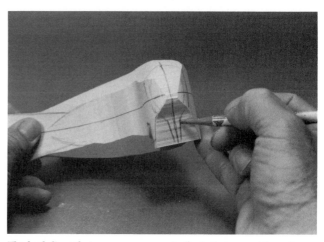

The beak lines that were sawn away in the last step must be redrawn. Shaping this area cannot be done with the bandsaw because the breast of the bird is right below it and would be cut away with the blade. Instead, a cutter will have to shape the profile.

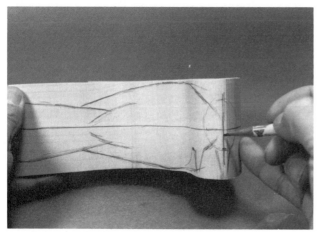

The top profile is cut out. Note that some of the lines made for the top view of the head have been removed and will have to be replaced.

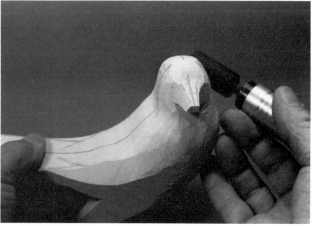

With an Arco rotary rasp and a Foredom, shape the head down to its approximate width. Continue onto the body.

Using the same rasp, work on the chest and flanks.

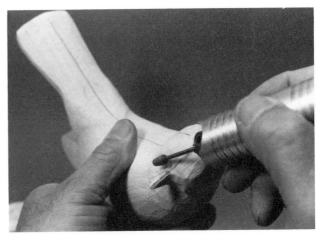

Establish the planes or top profiles of the beak.

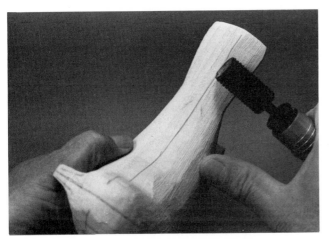

Shape the tail while maintaining the centerline.

The head has been shaped. The lower mandible has been reduced so that it seems to fit into the upper one. The eye channels have been established, their edges blended into the body. Also, the cheeks are in. Next, make a bib under the bird's beak with the ruby carver used in the previous steps.

After the body has been roughly shaped, use a pear-shaped number 23 ruby carver to establish the side profile of the beak.

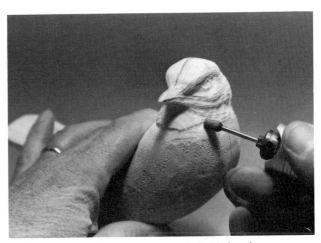

Another view of where the bib is carved with the ruby carver.

Draw in the circles for the 8-millimeter brown eyes.

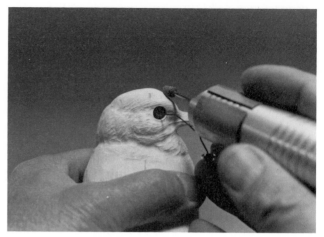

Make sure that the glass eyes fit flush into their holes.

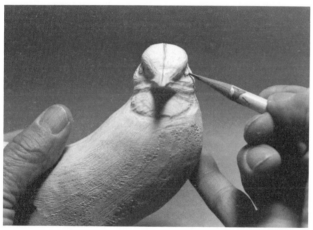

The robin's right eye is drawn in first, then its left eye. This procedure is for a right-handed person so that the bird can be worked head on to make sure one eye is not higher than the other.

A view of the bird's head at this stage.

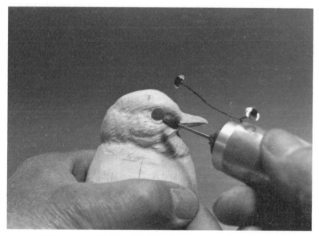

Make the eye holes with the ruby carver used previously.

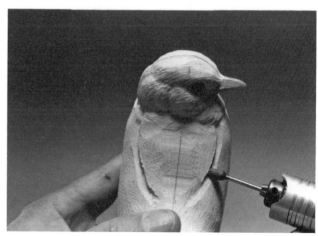

Draw in the robin's cape with the Foredom and number 23 ruby carver.

Blend the cape into the rest of the body so that there are no sharp edges.

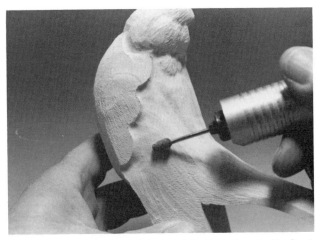

Round the depression off toward the rear of the bird, where the blending is less severe. Toward the front, there is more of a rise.

Establish the chest feathers where the chest overlaps the rest of the body. Note their scalloped shapes.

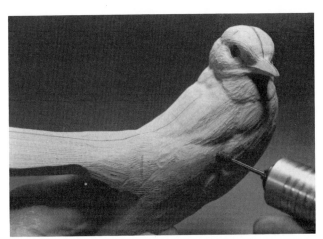

The chest has been blended on the other side.

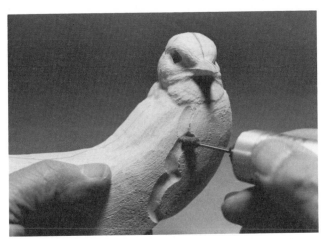

Using the Foredom and ruby carver like a pencil, make a continuous depression.

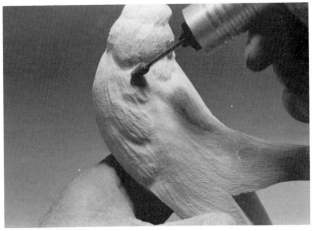

Make some muscles around the neck, plus the Muehlmatt bump, and blend them all into the body.

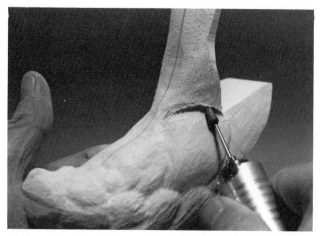

Dig into the rear of the bird where the secondary feathers will be. This makes the feathers slightly lower than the rump.

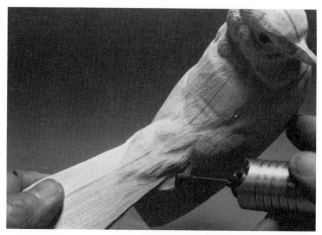

The rump feathers on this bird overlap the tail. The number 23 ruby carver can break them into small groups.

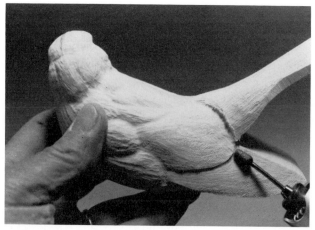

Lay out the primary group with the ruby carver. Ernie describes the strategy so far as shingling. The cape overlaps the secondaries, which overlap the primaries.

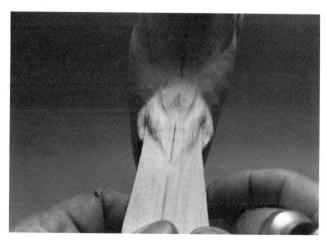

The completed rump feathers.

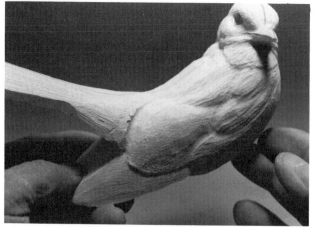

Blend the rump and tail together.

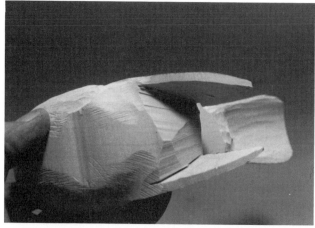

Use a bandsaw to cut away wood from between the primaries.

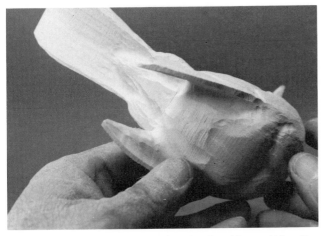

Remove excess wood from between the primaries with a carbide cutter, leaving the wings ⅛ inch thick.

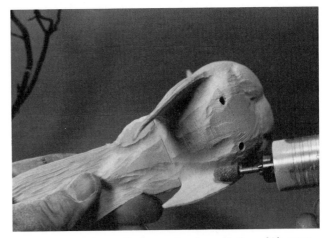

More work may have to be done on the wings with the carbide cutter.

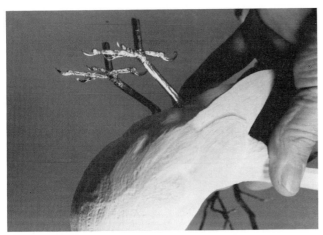

Determine where the cast feet go by holding them next to the body. Then drill holes for them.

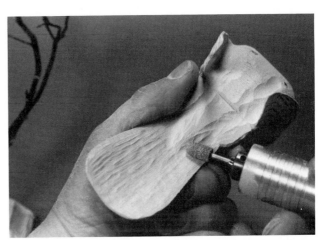

Reduce the thickness of the tail and make the under-tail coverts. The tail has to be reduced to about ⅛ inch in thickness.

Set the bird in place on its base. Make sure the bird looks comfortable, not leaning forward or backward. Ernie chose manzanita wood for part of the robin's habitat. The octagon walnut base was purchased from Birds of a Feather. (See appendix for address.)

Sand the wings smooth so that the feathers can be penciled in.

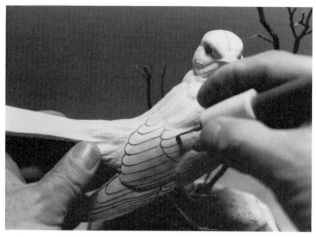

After drawing the feathers, burn them in lightly with a tight round tip.

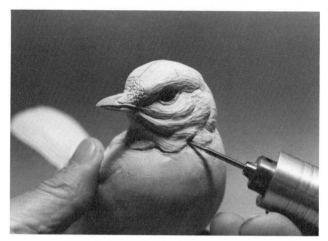

Undercut the bib slightly with the diamond bit.

With a barrel-shaped number 18 ruby carver that has had its end ground flat, layer the wing feathers slightly.

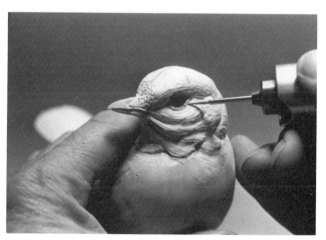

The same diamond bit can make lower eyelids.

With a needle-pointed diamond bit, define the feathers around the beak.

After the head is finished, do some defining on the over-tail coverts with the number 23 ruby carver, and define the individual tail feathers.

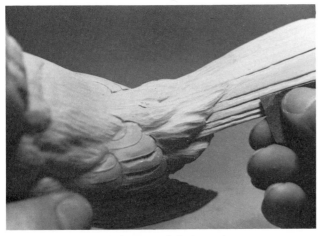

Sand smooth the cuts made in the previous step.

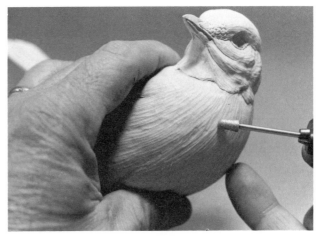

Sand the breast.

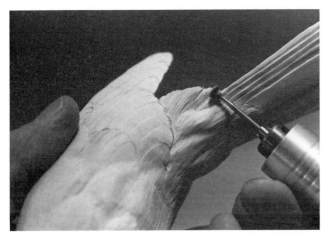

The shaggy, hairy feathers on the rump can be made with a grinding stone. Do the same underneath the rump.

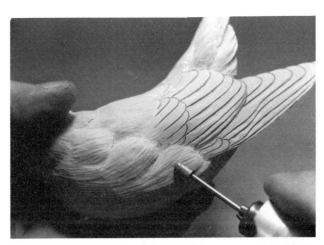

Work back toward the wing feathers, which are not sanded with the diamond bit.

With a bullet-shaped diamond bit, start going over the bird to leave a sanded yet irregular surface. Do this in the direction that the feathers lay.

Ernie did two robins at the same time. Here a comparison can be made between one sanded with the bit and one left smooth.

Another photo for study shows the sanded bird back on its base. It is now ready to be burned.

Turn the burning tool up slightly and shade each feather. This gives the illusion of the feathers being carved.

Draw in the chest feathers. Vary their sizes and stagger them, even though they do lay in rows.

Lay out the feathers under the chin.

Make a light burn with a zero setting.

After burning the feathers in lightly, go back with a skew tip and burn in the dark feather patterns.

After drawing in the head feathers, burn them dark with a skew tip. A light burn is not necessary.

Note that the feathers at the base of the neck lighten up slightly.

The burned head. The back of the head is not burned so darkly.

Burn the cape lightly and shade it with a slightly hotter heat setting, perhaps a number 1 setting on some burning tools.

Another view of the burned head. Note that the Muehlmatt bump is burned while a narrow area above each eye is not.

Burn the rump lightly and shade it.

The chest is also burned lightly and shaded.

Burn the underside of the tail lightly.

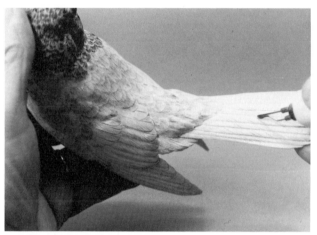

Burn the upper side of the tail lightly.

Before painting, a study skin can be used as a reference.

The wings are also burned lightly.

Coat all but the head of the bird with a thin mix of gesso and water. Ernie says this is necessary to enhance the solid colors on the robin. Burning alone, says Ernie, could not give a uniform color to the dark areas. Then make a gray out of a mixture of ultramarine blue and burnt umber, and paint each of the feathers in the wings. Shade them with a darker mix. This means two or three more washes on the upper side of each quill.

Paint the feathers on the cape and rump with the gray mix.

Again with ultramarine blue and burnt umber, do the underside of the tail, leaving white tips that are the result of the original undercoating of gesso and water. Some gray streaks are put on the underside of the rump.

Four or five more coats produce this effect on the wings. Then an overall wash blends everything together.

Breast feathers are outlined with white and washed over with burnt sienna.

More washes are applied to the cape and rump.

The light edges barely show through after applying the burnt sienna.

The finished bird.

Another view.

The beak has been painted with bronze yellow and washed with a mix of half matte medium, half water, and a small amount of warm black. The tip has perhaps twenty coats of this mix, with less applied toward the rear of the beak.

The finished bird on its base.

Under the rump.

The back of the robin.

Immature Robin

Downy Woodpecker

Downy Woodpecker

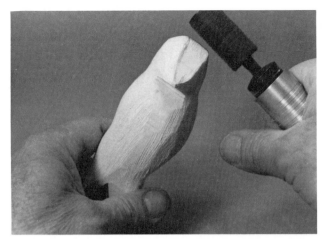

After the pattern is cut out from a piece of wood 2 inches thick, the top of the head is rough-shaped with a rotary rasp.

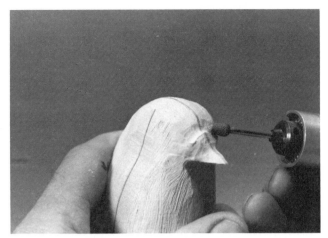

After the top profile of the beak has been shaped, do more work on the hairy patch over the beak.

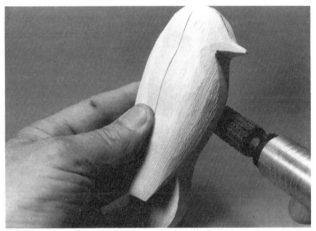

Rough-shape the body with the same rotary rasp.

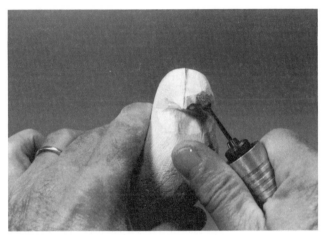

Work on the planes of the beak, looking at the bird from the front.

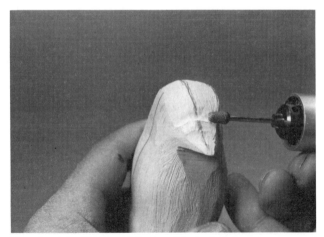

There is a tuft of feathers at the top of the beak that can be established with a pear-shaped number 23 ruby carver. Also work on the shape of the beak.

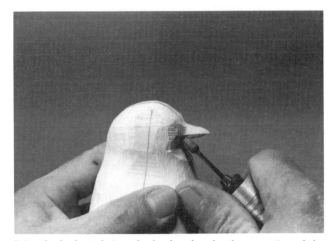

Bring the beak back into the head and make the separation of the mandibles by reducing the width of the lower one.

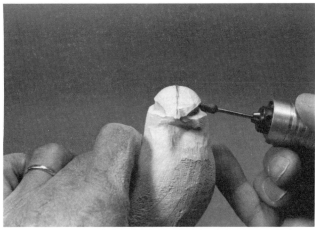

Make the eye depressions with the same ruby carver used in previous steps.

Blend the bumps into the rest of the head.

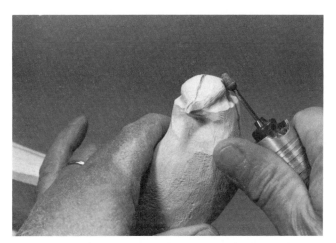

Remove the ledges or sharp edges on either side of the head.

Locate the holes for the 6-millimeter brown eyes.

Draw in the cheeks and the Muehlmatt bumps with the ruby carver.

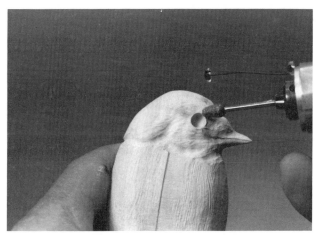

The number 23 ruby carver makes the holes for the eyes.

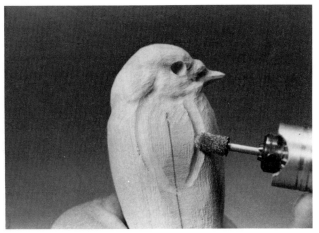

Go to the head with a carbide cutter. Ernie says he will use this at times because it removes the wood faster than a ruby carver and gives a wider cut.

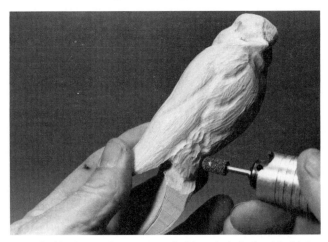

A tuft of feathers in this area is roughed in on both flanks of the bird.

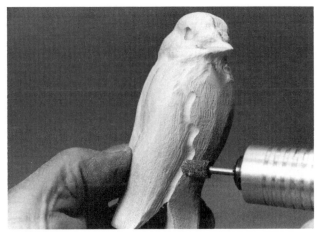

After blending the cape into the rest of the back, use the carbide cutter to establish where the chest feathers overlap the wings.

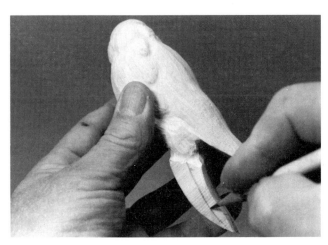

Draw the outside edge of the tail on both sides. The belly side of the cut will have to be removed.

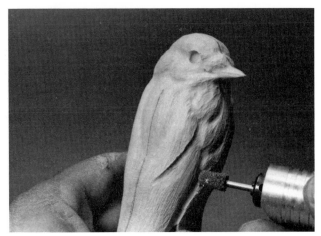

Blend the chest feathers into the rest of the body.

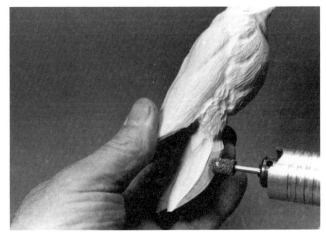

The wood is rounded over from one pencil mark to the other on the top side of the tail.

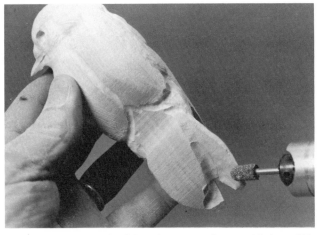

Working on the underside of the tail, carve wood away with the carbide cutter. Leave about ⅛ inch of wood. Also leave a thick area down the middle of the tail for the under-tail coverts.

The mounted bird. Woodpeckers usually sit with their tails flat against a tree, Ernie says.

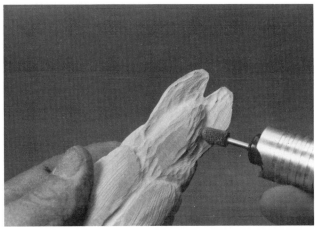

The wood left from the previous step makes up the under-tail coverts. The carbide cutter can give them a coarse, loose look.

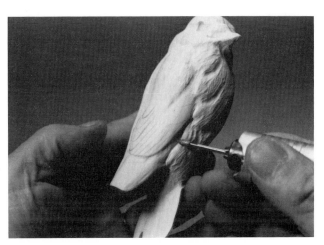

With a pointed number 19 ruby carver, do some defining and detailing on the tuft of flank feathers that sticks out slightly.

The woodpecker is attached to an upright piece of wood by mounting it on a wire post. Note the position of the hole for the wire.

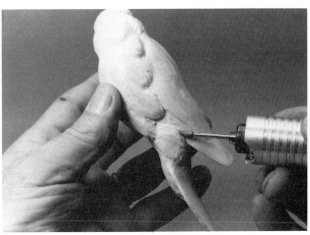

The tuft of feathers on the other side.

After drawing in the feathers of the primary and secondary groupings, outline them with a tight round burning tip.

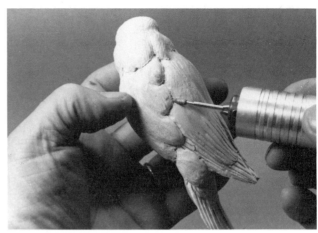

Where the breast feathers meet the body, undercut slightly with the ruby carver of the previous step.

Layer the feathers with a barrel-shaped number 18 ruby carver that has had its head ground flat.

Use a bullet-shaped diamond bit to sand the surface of the bird, working in the direction of the feathers.

Back to the head and a pointed number 19 ruby carver: undercut slightly the cheeks, the chin, and the Muehlmatt bump.

After the glass eyes are in place, press small balls of epoxy putty onto the eyes.

A wet finger can move the putty away from the glass.

After doing some coarse texturing with the edge of a small grinding stone on the white back patch of the bird, draw in the feather patterns on the head.

Use a knife blade to cut a slot at the front and the back of each eye.

Start burning the light areas on the head with a very low setting on the burning tool and a tight round tip.

A wet brush will shape the putty around the eyes.

Also burn the light areas under the chin.

Burn the dark areas with a skew tip. Notice the dark vermiculation on the chin.

Work on the breast and belly, which have a hairy texture. This can be done with ½-inch-long strokes.

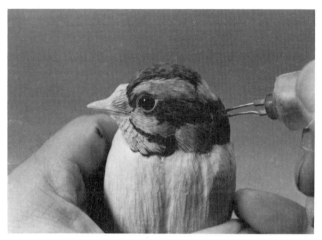

The back of the neck also has darkly burned areas.

On the downy woodpecker, hairy feathers prevail. Go over the stoned area on the back patch with the tight round and a low heat setting.

Burn light lines on the chest; avoid making them too uniform or straight.

Burn the dark areas on both sides of the white back patch. These too are somewhat hairy in appearance.

Outline the light and dark areas on the wings with a pencil.

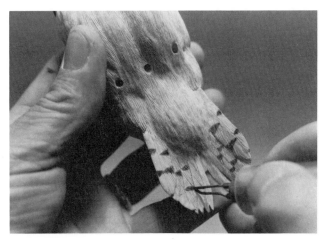

Burn under the tail lightly. Then burn in the patterns, which are a medium dark tone.

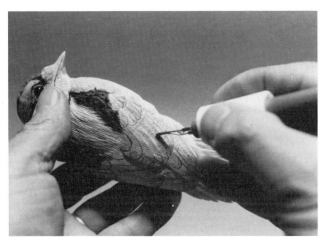

Burn the wings once lightly.

Burn lightly underneath the wings, which will later be a solid gray color.

Burn the dark areas with a hot setting and a skew tip.

Burn the upper-tail coverts, which are dark.

Three or four coats of watered-down gesso are applied to achieve the intensity of whiteness required.

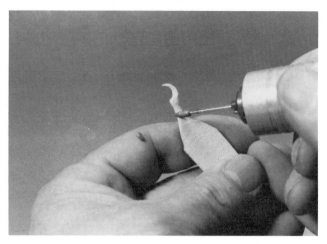

A pointed number 18 ruby carver shapes each toe.

Go over the wing bars and other white patterns with the gesso and water mix. The dark areas are gone over with a wash of warm black. Then a raw umber wash tones down the chalky appearance of the gesso. Little remains except the red patch on the back of the neck, which is cadmium red. The beak is washed with a mix of matte medium, water, and warm black.

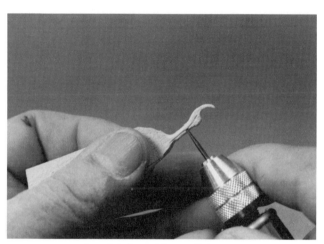

Detail work is done with a small diamond bit.

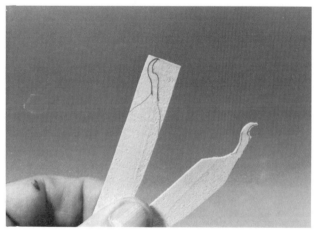

Instead of cast feet, wooden legs and toes can be made from ⅛-inch-thick pieces of tupelo. Four are needed for each leg.

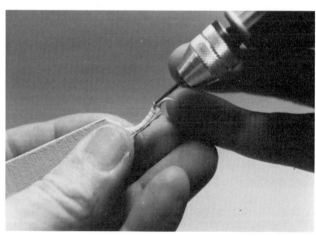

Another bit in a high-speed grinding tool makes the scales on each toe.

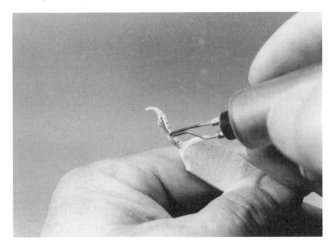

Burn in the small dots on the underside of each toe.

If the holes in the body are made deep enough, the legs can be adjusted by pulling them out or pushing them in with tweezers before being glued in place.

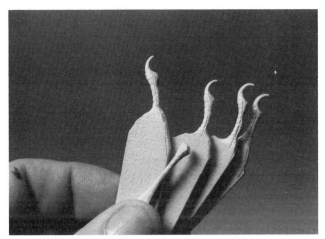

Four finished toes and one leg. For added strength, apply Krazy Glue to each piece.

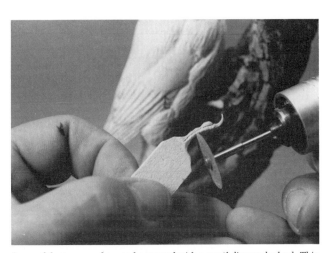

Some of the toes may have to be severed with a small diamond wheel. This will allow the toes to fit the branch better. Their edges, then, are mitered at an angle before the two parts are reattached.

Decide how the legs will fit into the bird and project out to the wood branch.

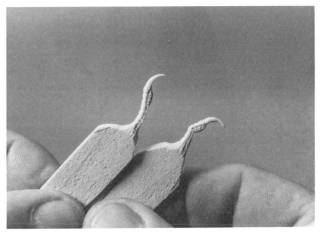

The toe at the right has been cut at its middle and reattached with glue, making for a toe with a greater bend in it to fit the branch.

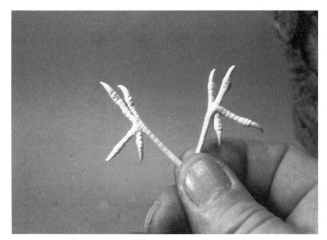

Two feet for the woodpecker. Toes have been glued to the legs.

The toes are in position, fitting the wood snugly. The feet are ready to be painted black.

A side view of the finished downy woodpecker.

A head-on view of the bird.

The back of the bird.

Evening Grosbeak

Evening Grosbeak

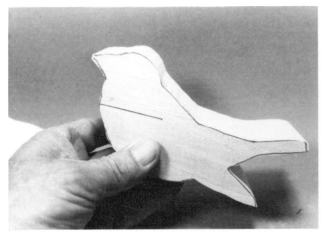

The side profile bandsawed to shape. Ernie says this is an interesting bird to do, especially for its colors.

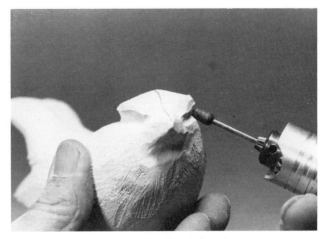

Carve in the eye channels with the ruby carver.

Establish the side profile of the beak with a pear-shaped number 23 ruby carver.

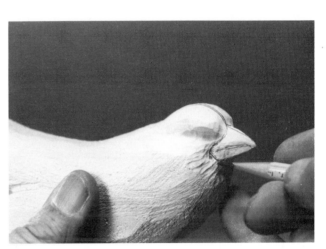

Bring the beak back into the head. A pencil will help here. Also establish the beak separation.

Work on the top profile with the ruby carver used previously.

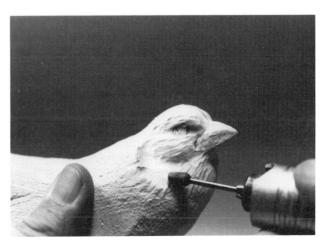

Make depressions on either side where the head meets the chest.

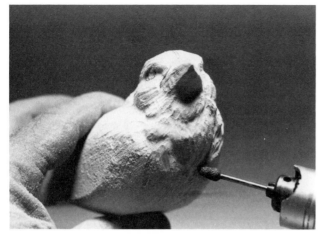

Muscles and bumps can be put on the chest with the number 23 ruby carver.

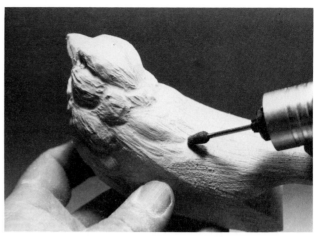

Draw in the cape with the ruby carver used previously and blend it into the rest of the body.

Draw in where the chest feathers overlap the wings.

Ernie calls this a wing bump. This too is blended into the body on both sides of the grosbeak.

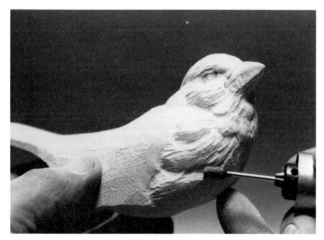

Blend the chest feathers into the wings. Also break up the chest feathers into clumps or groups.

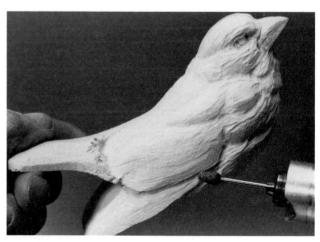

Step down an area between the primary and secondary groups on both sides of the bird.

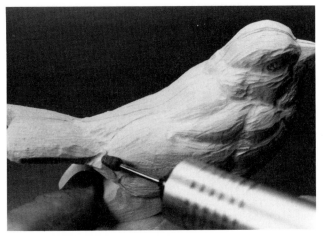

Define the area where the rump meets the tail.

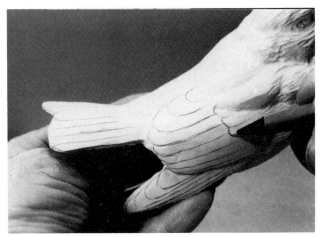

Draw in the secondary and primary feathers.

The wood between the primaries has to be bandsawed out. Then define the under-tail coverts.

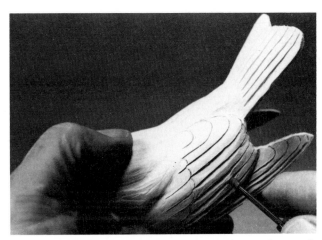

After burning in the wing feathers, layer them with a number 18 ruby carver.

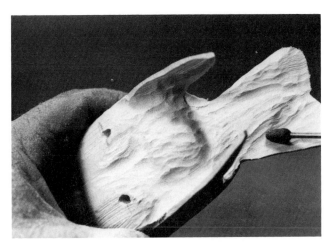

Blend the under-tail coverts into the tail feathers.

Define the separation between the upper and lower mandibles with a skew tip and burning tool.

The bird is ready for sanding.

Brush Krazy Glue on the beak to harden the wood.

Go over the entire body of the grosbeak with a diamond bit.

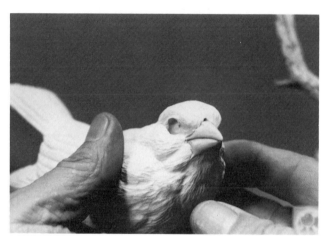

The beak has been hardened and sanded lightly. The eyes can now be put in.

The same diamond bit can put some irregular ends on the tail feathers.

The 8-millimeter brown eyes are in place. Also, the grosbeak has its cast feet in place, and it is on a branch.

The underside of the tail for study. Note how the under-tail coverts are broken up into clusters.

The cheeks are burned slightly darker than the forehead.

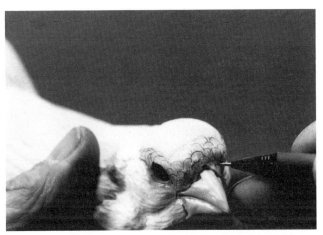

Draw small feathers on the top of the head.

Draw in the feathers on the top and back of the head.

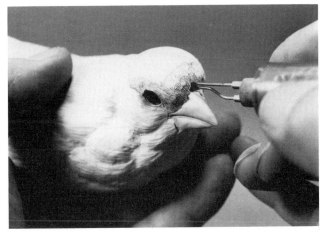

There is a light area on the forehead that becomes darker farther back. The light area is given a light burn.

The head feathers of the previous step are burned dark. Also notice the dark burn around the top of the beak and around the eyes.

Feathers under the chin are a medium shade between the light and dark feathers done so far. This is done with a moderate heat setting.

A light burn is done on the belly and under the tail.

The feathers on the neck are also given a medium burn.

The bird entirely burned.

The rest of the body is given a light burn.

Seal the bird with two-thirds lacquer and one-third lacquer thinner. Ernie uses a natural bristle brush for this. Nylon bristles will dissolve in lacquer.

Coat all but the dark areas on the head and the beak with a mix of gesso and water. The gesso accents the yellow tones to be applied later.

The secondaries are also painted with a mix of warm black and burnt umber. Ernie says he tried to maintain white feather edges, but they disappeared with the dark paint applications.

Apply cadmium yellow to the chest, the sides, the rump, and the back. Then put brown washes of raw umber and a small amount of ultramarine blue on the head, part of the back, and the chest. More coats will make areas progressively darker.

The finished bird. The beak, left a natural wood color, is given a light wash of bronze yellow and a light coat of gloss medium and water. The cast feet are washed with raw umber and matte medium.

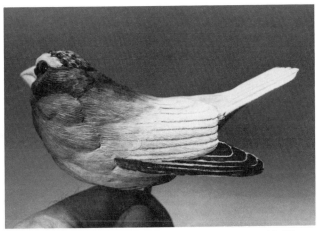

The primaries are painted with a mix of half warm black and half burnt umber. The tail is done the same way.

The finished grosbeak on its base.

Cardinal

Cardinal

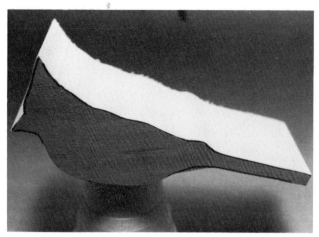

The side profile cut out on the bandsaw.

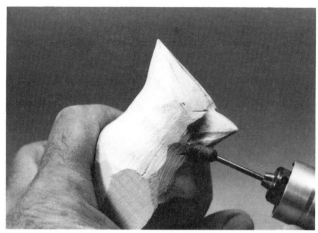

A pear-shaped number 23 ruby carver can bring the beak back into the head, depressing the corners of the mouth and building up the forehead.

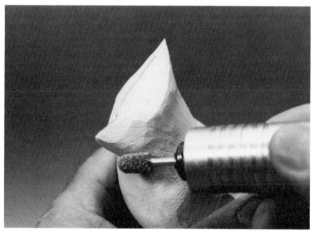

Rough-shaping of the head can be done with a carbide cutter.

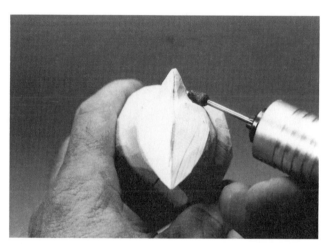

Looking at the head from the top can help with the shaping.

Comparing the side profile with a study skin may help, especially with the beak. Based on what he saw, Ernie had to reshape the wooden beak.

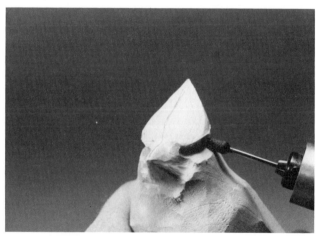

Make the eye channels with the same ruby carver.

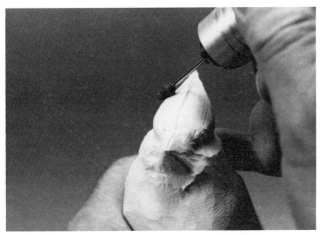

Round off the top of the head above the eye channels.

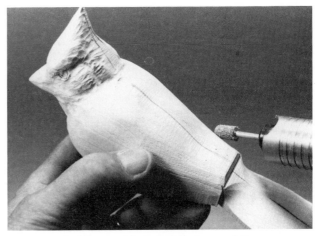

Round off the rest of the body with a heavy carbide cutter.

Define the cheeks, drawing them in with the pear-shaped number 23 ruby carver.

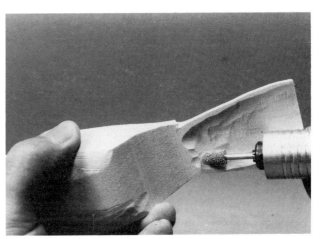

Hollow out the underside of the tail.

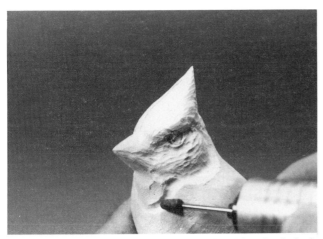

Round off the sharp edges of the cheeks and make a bib under the beak. Round that off also. At this stage the eyes can be located.

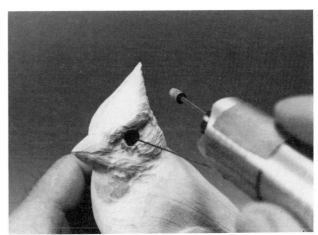

Drill in the eye holes with the number 23 ruby carver.

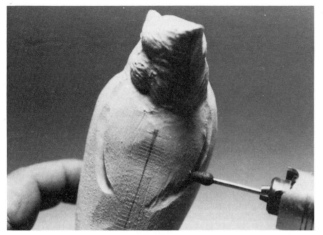

Draw in the cape with the same ruby carver used previously.

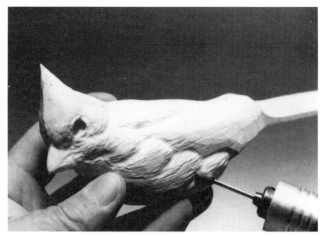

Blend the chest feathers into the rest of the body, but break them into clusters. The same number 23 ruby carver can be used.

Round off the cape, blending it into the rest of the body.

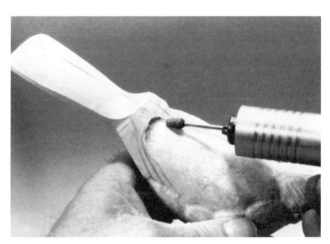

Depress an area where the secondary wing feathers cut into the rump. The high area between those feathers and the tail will have to be removed.

Draw in the chest feathers with a pencil where they overlap the wings.

Define the area where the primaries and the rump meet.

Draw in the feathers on the primary and secondary groupings with a pencil.

Break the chest feathers into clumps or groups with the number 23 ruby carver.

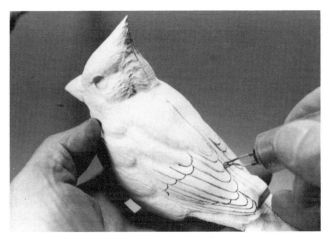

Burn around the edge of each feather with a tight round burning tip.

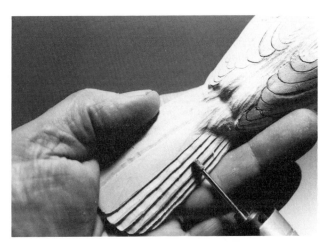

Lay out the tail feathers and layer them with a flattened number 18 ruby carver.

A skew tip and burning pen can separate the upper and lower mandibles of the cardinal. Note that the beak separation has a definite dip to it.

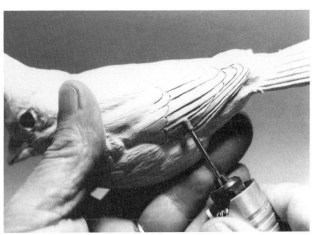

The barrel-shaped ruby carver can separate the wing feathers.

A small, fine grinding stone in a high-speed grinding tool can do the hairy feathers on the face. The one Ernie uses runs at 35,000 rpm.

The eyes are set in and surrounded with epoxy putty. Note the notches in the lower lid done before the putty dries. A sharp tool such as a knife can make these.

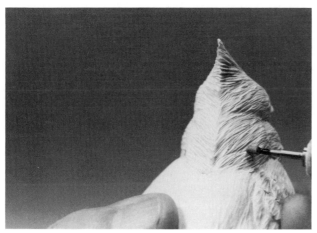

The same stone and grinder will do the feathers on the back of the cardinal's head.

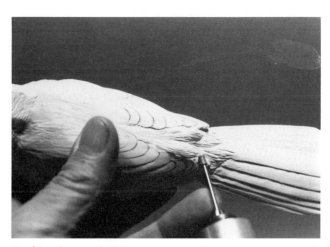

For doing the rump feathers, Ernie suggests using the barrel-shaped ruby carver and Foredom.

The head details. Ernie credits the fineness of the texturing to the high-speed grinder.

Burning begins with the head. Use a light burn.

A tight round tip and a very low setting on the burning tool does the head area.

Lay out the feathers with a pencil, varying their widths and staggering them.

Ernie describes these darkly burned areas as the bib and mask of the cardinal.

Burn lightly with a tight round.

After burning the head, go to the rest of the bird, all of which is burned lightly and shaded in some areas.

Shade each feather with a slightly hotter setting.

Burning on the secondary coverts.

Seal the bird with two-thirds lacquer and one-third lacquer thinner, then give it a light coat of gesso and water.

The secondary and primary feathers have only one light burn.

Start with washes of cadmium red for the head and breast. A mix of cadmium red, burnt umber, and ultramarine blue is used on the back.

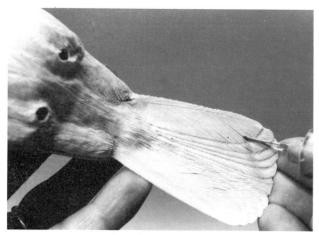

Burn the underside of the tail lightly.

A darker mix of cadmium red, burnt umber, and ultramarine blue is used on the wing feathers. Leave the edges white.

Use the same dark mix on the tail. Under the tail is a mix of burnt umber and ultramarine blue.

The finished bird. The legs can be done with just raw umber to make a brown color. The beak is a reddish orange. Ernie suggests using light washes of cadmium red with bronze yellow. Matte medium can be used to give the beak a shiny look.

Immature Cardinal

Blue Jay Family

Blue Jay Family

This project needs two patterns. The mother jay is one; the babies underneath make up the other. Ernie calls this a composite pattern.

The pattern of the mother jay and some details drawn on the wood.

Lay the pattern out on a piece of 4-inch-thick tupelo, and cut it out on the bandsaw.

Start lowering the wood around the mother's head, which will be the highest area on the carving.

Lay out just the pattern of the mother bird on top of the bandsawed wood.

Carving starts on the mother's head, again reducing wood around it. This can be done with a large carbide cutter.

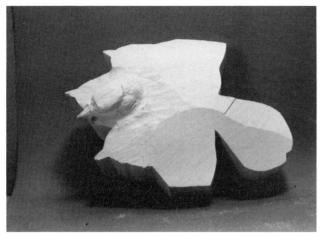

The head is well defined at this stage.

Define muscles on the mother's back and define the over-tail coverts.

Another view of the head brought out of the wood. Note how the tail has been lowered with the bandsaw.

Back to the babies for more work on their bodies. Ernie says this is a process of making sure all the bodies fit together. Wood must be taken away with care.

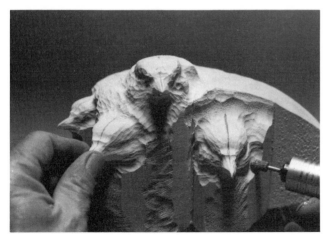

Rough out each of the babies' heads.

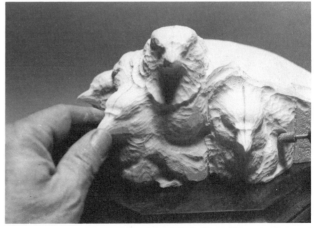

Determine where the wings and feet of the babies will go. Again, wood must be removed slowly and carefully. Also establish the bib on the mother blue jay.

Relieve wood underneath the mother's wings and tail. Leave enough wood for each of the bodies underneath.

Work on the beaks can be done with a ruby carver or a diamond bit.

More defining underneath the piece. Note that one of the babies' tails has been shaped.

The blue jay family so far. Note the beak separations, the eye holes, the wings on the babies, and the details on the mother's face.

Do more shaping where the bodies touch each other. Ernie says a wing pokes into another bird or one chest meets another.

After drawing the feather patterns on the mother, outline them with a burning pen and a tight round tip.

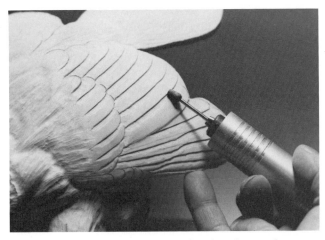

The feathers can be layered with a pear-shaped number 23 ruby carver.

Unlike those on the wings, the tail feathers will have raised quills. Note the layout.

Sand the feathers smooth. This can be done with a piece of sandpaper in a split mandrel or steel spindle.

Raising the quills is done with a ball-shaped diamond bit.

The wing feathers carved and sanded. The same procedure will be followed for the tail.

The same diamond bit can sand smooth the rest of the bird, leaving a smooth but irregular surface. Do not use this bit on the wing or tail feathers.

Details on the underside of the wing and tail feathers.

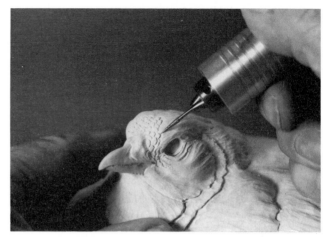

Fine-tuning is done with a needle-pointed diamond bit.

To achieve a coarse look on the breasts of the babies, use the edge of a small grinding stone.

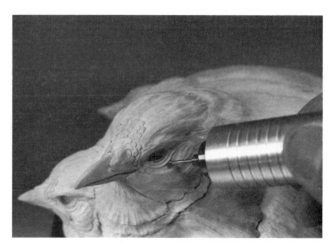

Work around the eyes is done with a ball-shaped diamond bit.

Layering the head feathers on the birds begins with a pointed number 19 ruby carver.

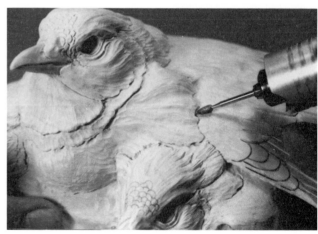

Undercut where the breast of the mother bird meets her wings. Use a pointed number 19 ruby carver.

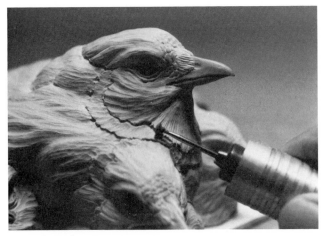

Use the edge of a grinding stone under the chin of the mother jay to achieve a coarse look. Do the same above the mother's beak.

The eyes have to be set in with glue before the epoxy putty is applied around them.

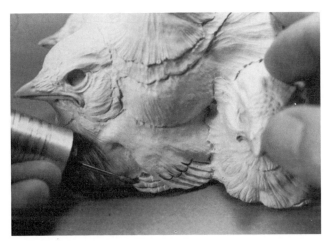

With the pointed number 19 ruby carver, define the babies' toes.

Make a light burn on the heads with a tight round tip.

Apply Krazy Glue to all the beaks, and lightly sand them after the glue has dried.

A skew tip will burn the dark rings around the heads and the dark patches around the blue jays' eyes.

Burn lightly on the mother's back and shoulders. These burns should look hairy.

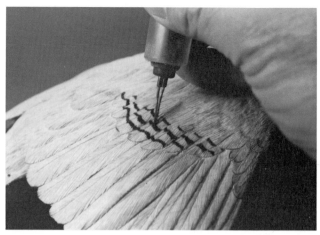

The secondary coverts have dark bars. These will have to be done with a sharp burning tip and a high heat setting on the burning tool.

Burn the primary and secondary feathers with the tight round. Splits can be put in by increasing the pressure on the tip.

Make long, hairy feathers on the rump with a tight round.

The burning nearly completed on the back and the wings.

Burn lightly under the tail.

The top side of the tail also has bars that must be burned dark.

Ernie chose a round walnut base for the blue jay family. A copper peg and a piece of square tubing both help position the grouping and allow it to be removed.

Scallop-shaped bars are made on the secondary feathers.

The birds on their base ready to be painted.

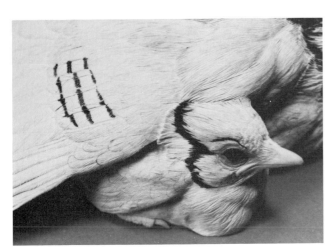

Light burning is done on the babies.

Seal the birds with a mix of two-thirds clear lacquer and one-third lacquer thinner.

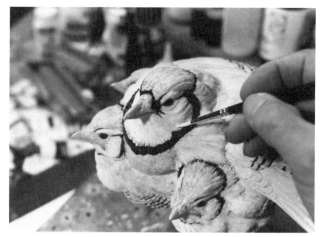

Lightly coat all areas not burned dark with watered-down gesso, but apply several more coats to the very white areas such as under the mother's beak.

The primaries need two coats of gesso.

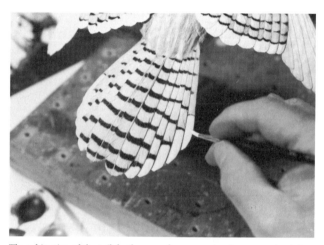

The white tips of the tail feathers need more coats of gesso, perhaps four coats.

Using ultramarine blue and burnt umber in different proportions will result in a variety of colors from bright blue to a gray blue to a brownish gray. Ernie says the heads of the babies are grayer than the mother's head. The chest of the mother is a brownish gray.

The tips of the secondary feathers also need more coats of gesso.

The mother's back is a grayish blue.

The first few feathers in the secondary group are a bright blue. A straight application of ultramarine blue can be used here.

The upper half is darker than the lower half of each primary feather.

As the secondary feathers progress out toward the primaries, they become darker, almost a blackish blue.

The underside of the wing feathers is painted a dark blue, as is the tail. The tips of the tail feathers are left white.

The primaries are shaded differently on either side of each quill.

The inside top of each tail feather is a lighter blue than the outside portion. A wet-on-wet method can be used. This means applying darker washes while the lighter ones are still wet. Blending with noticeable transitions will occur owing to the wetness.

Ernie says each feather must be painted individually. Then one or two washes of a mix of ultramarine blue and burnt umber are applied to tone down the colors on the tail and bring the color variations together.

Another view of the finished birds.

The finished birds. Note that the mother's beak is much darker than the babies' beaks. But all coats applied to all the beaks are mixed with matte medium.

Bluejay

Appendix

A Sampling of Competitions and Exhibitions

This list was compiled from *Wildlife Carving and Collecting Magazine*. Addresses indicate where to get further information.

Annapolis Wildfowl Carving and Art Exhibition
1144 Riverboat Court
Annapolis, MD 21401
Carving and art exhibits are featured in this late January show.

The California Open and Wildfowl Arts Festival
4351 Whittle Ave.
Oakland, CA 94602
Held in mid-February, this show attracts 400 carvers and exhibitors and 8,000 visitors.

Canadian National Decoy Carvers Competition
Sportsmans Association
61 Edgehill Rd.
Islington, Ontario
M9A 4N1
This show is held in mid-March with some 300 entries of wildfowl carvings.

U.S. National Decoy Show
5 Flint Rd.
Amity Harbor, NY 11701
Held in middle to late March, it is the oldest show of its kind in this country.

World Championship Wildfowl Carving Competition
The Ward Foundation
655 S. Salisbury Blvd.
Salisbury, MD 21801
Held in Ocean City, Maryland, in late April, this show features some 800 carvers and attracts around 16,000 visitors. This three-day event is a must for anyone interested in bird carving.

Clayton Duck Decoy and Wildlife Art Show
P.O. Box 292
Clayton, NY 13624
Held in July, this show offers auctions, demonstrations, painting, and carving contests.

International Decoy Contest
P.O. Box 406
Davenport, IA 52805
This is an early August show, which attracts over 100 carvers and some 5,000 visitors.

Loyalhanna Wildlife Art Festival
Loyalhanna Watershed Assoc.
P.O. Box 561
Ligonier, PA 15658
Held in September, the show offers demonstrations, wildlife films, and an auction.

Louisiana Wildlife Festival
3112 Octavia St.
New Orleans, LA 70125
Held in New Orleans, this September show features some
300 carvers and exhibitors with some 10,000 visitors.

Leigh Yawkey Woodson Art Museum "Birds in Art"
Exhibition
Leigh Yawkey Woodson Art Museum
Franklin and Twelfth Sts.
Wausau, WI 54401
This show may come the closest to treating bird sculpture
as an art form. It is held early September to early
November.

North American Wildfowl Carving Championship
4510 Kircaldy Rd.
Bloomfield Hills, MI 48013
Point Mouille State Game Area is the site for this key show
in late September, which attracts nearly 300 carvers.

The Ward Foundation Wildfowl Carving and Art
Exhibition
The Ward Foundation
P.O. Box 703
Salisbury, MD 21801
This early October show, held in Salisbury, is not a
competition but an exhibition of carvings and flat work art.
Some 150 artists attend with some 9,000 visitors.

New England Woodcarvers Festival and Competition
Valley Shore Waterfowlers
43 Ridgeview Circle
Guilford, CT 06437
Held in late October or early November, this show made
its debut in 1985.

Easton Waterfowl Festival
P.O. Box 929
Easton, MD 21654
This is an early November town-wide wildfowl art
exhibition, features 450 carvers and exhibitors, and attracts
some 25,000 visitors. A number of the carvers in this book
and in *How to Carve Wildfowl* exhibit their work there.

Pennsylvania Wildlife Art Festival
R.D. #1
P.O. Box 128A
Glen Rock, PA 17327
This show is held in York in mid-November with a wide
variety of decorative carvings featured.

Cajun Hunters Festival
Rt. 2
P.O. Box 337
Cut Off, LA 70345
Held in the Bayou Centroplex in Galliano, this show
features over 100 carvers and exhibitors with some 5,000
visitors.

Sources for Supplies

Al's Decoy Supplies
27 Connaught Ave.
London, Ontario N5Y 3A4
CANADA
519-451-4729

Albert Constantine & Sons, Inc.
2050 Eastchester Rd.
Bronx, NY 10461
212-792-1600

American Sales Co.
Box 741
Reseda, CA 91335
213-881-2808

Big Sky Carvers
8256 Huffine Ln.
Bozeman, MT 59715
406-586-0008

Buck Run Carvings
Box 151, Gully Rd.
Aurora, NY 13026
315-364-8414

Canadian Woodworker Ltd.
1391 St. James St.
Winnipeg, Manitoba R3H 0Z1
CANADA
204-786-3196

The Carver's Barn
P.O. Box 686
Rte. 28
Hearth & Eagle Shopping Plaza
South Yarmouth, MA 02664

Carvers Corner
153 Passaic St.
Garfield, NJ 07026
201-472-7511

Chez La Rogue
Rt. 3, Box 148
Foley, AL 36535
205-943-1237

Craft Cove, Inc.
2315 W. Glen Ave.
Peoria, IL 61614
309-692-8365

CraftWoods
10921 York Rd.
Cockeysville, MD 21030
301-667-9663

Curt's Waterfowl Corner
123 Le Boeuf St.
Montegut, LA 70377
504-594-3012

The Duck Butt Boys
P.O. Box 2051
Metairie, LA 70004
504-443-3797

Electric & Tool Service Co.
19442 Conant Ave.
Detroit, MI 48234
313-366-3830

P.C. English Enterprises
P.O. Box 7937
Lafayette Blvd.
Fredericksburg, VA 22404
703-371-1306

Exotic Woods Inc.
2483 Industrial Street
Burlington, Ontario L7P 1A6
CANADA
416-335-8066

Feather Merchants
279 Boston Post Rd.
Madison, CT 06443
203-245-1231

The Fine Tool Shops, Inc.
P.O. Box 1262
20 Backus Ave.
Danbury, CT 06810
800-243-1037

The Foredom Electric Co.
Rt. 6
Bethel, CT 06801
203-792-8622

Forest Products
P.O. Box 12
Avon, OH 44011
216-937-5630

Garrett Wade
161 Avenue of the Americas
New York, NY 10013
800-212-2942

Gerry's Tool Shed
1111 Flint Road
Unit 6
Downsview, Ontario M3J 3C7
CANADA
416-665-6677

Gesswein
Woodworking Products Division
255 Hancock Ave.
P.O. Box 3998
Bridgeport, CT 06605
800-243-4466
203-366-5400

J. H. Kline Carving Shop
R.D. 2, Forge Hill Rd.
Manchester, PA 17345
717-266-3501

Ken Jones
P.O. Box 563
Salem, NH 03079

Kent's Woodshed
625 W. Main
Broussard, LA 70518
318-837-9470

Lee Valley Tools Ltd.
2680 Queensview Dr.
Ottawa, Ontario K2B 8J9
CANADA
613-596-0350

Lewis Tool and Supply Co.
912 West 8th St.
Loveland, CO 80537
303-663-4405

Little Mountain Carving Supply
Rt. 2, Box 1329
Front Royal, VA 22630
703-662-6160

L. I. Woodcarvers Supply
60 Glouster Rd.
Massapequa, NY 11758
516-799-7999

McGray Wildlife Sculpture
6553 Panton St.
Kilbride, Ontario L0P 1G0
CANADA
416-335-2512

Master Paint Systems
P.O. Box 1320
Loganville, GA 30249
800-334-8012

Montana Decoy Co.
Route 1
Box 251
Wilsall, MT 59086
406-578-2235

Northwest Carving Supply
P.O. Box 5211
216 West Ridge
Bozeman, MT 59715
406-587-8057

Plympton Wildlife Studios
David Coelho
244 Brook Street
Plympton, MA 02367
617-585-9107

Denny Rogers
309 Daisy Ln.
Normal, IL 61761
309-452-8005

Ross Tool Co.
257 Queen Street, West
Toronto, Ontario M5V 1Z4
CANADA
416-598-2498

Sand-Rite Mfg. Co.
1611 N. Sheffield Ave.
Chicago, IL 60614
312-642-7287

Seto Co., Inc.
"Serabian Tool Co."
P.O. Box 148
195 Highway 36
West Keansburg, NJ 07734
201-495-0040

Tool Bin
10575 Clark Rd.
Davisburg, MI 48019
313-625-0390

Troy Woodcraft
301 Scottsdale Dr.
Troy, MI 48084
313-689-1997

Veasey Studios
955 Blue Ball Rd.
Elkton, MD 21921
301-392-3850

Joe Veracke and Assoc.
P.O. Box 48962
Chicago, IL 60648
312-824-9696

Valley Carving Studio
1720 Ellington Rd.
South Windsor, CT 06074

Warren Tool Co.
Rt. 1 14AS
Rhinebeck, NY 12572
914-876-7817

Welbeck Sawmill Ltd.
R. R. 2
Durham, Ontario N0G 1R0
CANADA
519-369-2144

Wildlife Carvings Supply
317 Holyoke Ave.
Beach Haven, NJ 08008
609-492-1871

Wildlife Woodcarvers
Avian Art, Inc.
4288 Staunton Dr.
Swartz Creek, MI 48473
313-732-6300

Wood Carvers Supply Co.
3056 Excelsior Blvd.
Minneapolis, MN 55416
612-927-7491

Wood Carvers Supply, Inc.
P.O. Box 8928
Norfolk, VA 23503
804-583-8928

Woodcraft Supply
41 Atlantic Ave.
Box 4000
Woburn, MA 01888
800-225-1153

Wood-Regan Instrument Co.
Vermiculation Pen
107 Forest St.
Montclair, NJ 07042

Books
Books Plus
133 St. Joseph's Blvd.
P.O. Box 731
Lodi, NJ 07644
201-777-3033

Highwood Bookshop
P.O. Box 1246
Traverse City, MI 49684
616-271-3898

Burning Tools
Chesterfield Craft Shop
P.O. Box 208
Chesterfield, NJ 08620

Colwood Electronics
715 Westwood Ave.
Long Branch, NJ 07740
201-222-2568

Hot Tools
7 Hawkes St.
P.O. Box 615
Marblehead, MA 01945
617-639-1000

The Detail Master
Leisure Time Products
2 Hillview Dr.
Barrington, IL 60010

Carving Knives
Cheston Knotts
106 S. Ford Ave.
Wilmington, DE 19805
302-652-5046

Lominack Knives
P.O. Box 1189
Abingdon, VA 24210
703-628-6591

Makepeace
1482 Maple Ave.
Paoli, PA 19301
215-644-6318

Cast Feet
Richard Delise
920 Springwood Dr.
West Chester, PA 19380
215-436-4377

Wildlife Studios
244 Brook St.
Plympton, MA 02367

Cast Study Bills
Bob Bolle
26421 Compson
Roseville, MI 48066
313-773-3153

Bob Miller
General Delivery
Evergreen, LA 71333
318-346-4270

Oscar Johnston Wildlife Gallery
Rt. 2, Box 1224
Smith River, CA 95567
707-487-4401

John W. Sebalusky
P.O. Box 1062
Bensalem, PA 19020

Glass Eyes
Carvers Eye
P.O. Box 16692
Portland, OR 97216

Eyes
9630 Dundalk
Spring, TX 77379
713-376-2897

Hutch Decoy Carving Ltd.
7715 Warsaw Ave.
Glen Burnie, MD 21061
301-437-2501

Schoepfer Eyes
138 West 31st St.
New York, NY 10001
212-736-6934

Robert J. Smith
14900 W. 31st Ave.
Golden, CO 80401
303-278-1828

Tohickon Glass Eyes
P.O. Box 15
Erwinna, PA 18920
800-441-5983

Grinding Tool Burrs and Accessories
Pfingst & Company, Inc.
P.O. Box 377
South Plainfield, NJ 07080

Gamzon Bros. Inc.
21 W. 46th St.
New York, NY 10036
212-719-2550
800-223-6464

Molded Birds
Greenwing Enterprises
Rt. 2, Box 731-B
Chester, MD 21619
301-643-3717

StudyKast
Godin Art. Inc.
P.O. Box 62
Brantford, Ontario N3T 5N3
CANADA
519-756-1613

Paints and Brushes
Jim and Beebe Hopper
731 Beech Ave.
Chula Vista, CA 92010
619-420-8766

Christian J. Hummul Co.
404 Brooklets Ave.
Easton, MD 21601
301-636-2232

Windsor & Newton Inc.
555 Winsor Dr.
Secaucus, NJ 07094
201-864-9100

Ruby Carvers
Elkay Products Co.
1506 Sylvan Glade
Austin, TX 78745
512-441-1155

Taxidermists
American Wildlife Studio
Box 71, Tuckahoe Rd.
Dorothy, NJ 08317
609-476-2941

Cooper Taxidermy
County Road 50W.
Valparaiso, IN
462-0643

Frank Newmyer
5783 Garthby
Union Lake, MI 48085
313-363-1243

Mike's Taxidermy Studio
5019 Lolly Lane
Perry Hall, MD 21128
301-256-0860

Richard Smoker
19 W. Pear St.
Crisfield, MD 21817
301-968-3044

Video Cassettes
"Bird Carving: Art in Detail".
Windsor Promotions, Inc.
127 Bruckner Blvd.
New York, NY 10454

Waterfowl Video Tapes
The Duck Blind
8721-B Gull Rd.
Richland, MI 49083
616-629-9198

"World Championship Video Series featuring Pat Godin"
Georgetowne, Inc.
P.O. Box 625
Bethel Park, PA 15102

Robert S. Bennett
Fredericksburg, VA
703-898-0375

Wildfowl Photos
Cardinal Carvers Supply
P.O. Box 571
Houma, LA 70361

John E. Heintz, Jr.
6609 S. River Rd.
Marine City, MI 48039
313-765-5059

Larry Stevens
3005 Pine Spring Rd.
Falls Church, VA 22042
703-560-5771

Wooden Bases
Birds of a Feather
Box 386
41 Edstrom Rd.
Marlborough, CT 06447
203-295-9469

Ken Thomas Bases
1909 Woodstream Dr.
York, PA 17402

Display Cases
Rioux's Wildlife in Wood and Pewter
P.O. Box 3008
Syracuse, NY 13220-3008

Bibliography

Alcorn, Gordon Dee. *Owls*. Prentice Hall Press, 1986.

Audubon, John James. *The Birds of America*. Crown Publisher, 1966.

Austin, Oliver L. *Birds of the World*. Golden Press, 1961.

Aymar, Gordon. *Bird Flight*. Dodd, Mead & Co.

Beebe, C. William. *The Bird: Its Form and Function*. Dover Publications, 1965.

Boulton, Rudyard. *Traveling with the Birds*. M.A. Donahue & Co., 1960.

Boyer, Trevor, and Burton, Philip. *Vanished Eagles*. Dodd, Mead & Co., 1981.

Burk, Bruce. *Game Bird Carving*. Winchester Press, 1982.

Burke, Ken. *How to Attract Birds*. Ortho Books, 1983.

Burton, John A., ed. *Owls of the World*. E.P. Dutton & Co., 1973.

Campbell, Bruce, ed. *The Pictorial Encyclopedia of Birds*. Paul Hamlyn, 1967.

Campbell, W. D. *Birds of Town and Village*. Country Life Books, 1965.

Casey, Peter N. *Birds of Canada*. Discovery Books, 1984.

Clement, Roland C. *The Living World of Audubon*. Grosset & Dunlop, 1974.

Coleman, Bruce. *Birds*. Crescent Books.

Coles, Charles, and Pledger, Maurice. *Game Birds*. Dodd, Mead & Co., 1985.

Cruickshank, Allan D. *Cruickshank's Photographs of Birds of America*. Dover Publications, 1977.

Dossenbach, Hans D. *The Family Life of Birds*. McGraw-Hill Book Co., 1971.

Dougall, Robert, and Ede, Basil. *Basil Ede's Birds*. Van Nostrand, Reinhold, 1981.

Duval, Paul. *The Art of Glen Loates*. Cerebrus Publishing Co., 1977.

Eckert, Allan W., and Karalus, Karl F. *The Wading Birds of North America*. Doubleday, 1981.

Farrand, John, Jr., ed. *The Audubon Society Master Guide to Birding*. 3 vols. Alfred A. Knopf, 1983.

Fisher, James, and Peterson, Roger Tory. *World of Birds*. Rev. Crescent Books.

Forbush, Edward H., and May, John R. *A Natural History of American Birds of Eastern and Central North America*. Bramhall House, 1955.

Gilley, Wendell H. *The Art of Bird Carving*. Hillcrest Publishers, 1972.

Godfrey, W. Earl. *The Birds of Canada*. National Museums of Canada, 1966.

Gooders, John. *Collins British Birds*. William Collins Sons & Co., 1982.

Gullion, Gordon. *Grouse of the North Shore*. Willow Creek Press, 1984.

Harrison, Colin. *A Field Guide to the Nests, Eggs and Nestlings of North American Birds.* Collins, 1978.

Harrison, Hal H. *Wood Warblers' World.* Simon and Schuster, 1984.

Hosking, Eric. *Eric Hosking's Waders.* Pelham Books, 1983.

James, Ross. *Glen Loates Birds of North America.* Prentice Hall of Canada, 1979.

Jeklin, Isidor, and Waite, Donald E. *The Art of Photographing North American Birds.* Whitecap Books, 1984.

Johnsgard, Paul A. *The Plovers, Sandpipers, and Snipes of the World.* University of Nebraska Press, 1981.

————. *Grouse and Quails of North America.* University of Nebraska Press, 1973.

————. *North American Game Birds of Upland and Shoreline.* University of Nebraska Press, 1975.

Landsdowne, J. Fenwick. *Birds of the West Coast.* Houghton Mifflin Co., 1980.

————. *Birds of the West Coast II.* Houghton Mifflin Co., 1980.

Landsdowne, J. Fenwick, and Livingston, John A. *Birds of the Eastern Forest.* Houghton Mifflin Co., 1968.

————. *Birds of the Eastern Forest II.* Houghton Mifflin Co., 1970.

————. *Birds of the Northern Forest.* Houghton Mifflin Co., 1966.

Laycock, George. *The Birdwatcher's Bible.* Doubleday & Co., 1976.

Leopold, Aldo. *A Sand County Almanac.* Oxford University Press, 1968.

Line, Les. *Audubon Society Book of Wild Birds.* Harry N. Abrams, 1976.

Lyttle, Richard B. *Birds of North America.* Gallery Books, 1983.

McKenny, Margaret. *Birds in the Garden.* The University of Minnesota Press, 1939.

Marcham, Frederick George, ed. *Louis Agassiz Fuertes & the Singular Beauty of Birds.* Harper & Row Publishers, 1971.

Matthiessen, Peter. *The Shore Birds of North America.* Viking Press, 1967.

Mitchell, Alan. *Lambart's Birds of Shore and Estuary.* Scribners, 1979.

————. *Field Guide to Birds of North America.* National Geographic Society, 1983.

————. *Stalking Birds with Color Camera.* National Geographic Society, 1961.

————. *Water, Prey and Game Birds.* National Geographic Society, 1965.

Mohrhardt, David. *Bird Reference Drawings.* Publication of David Mohrhardt, 314 N. Bluff, Berrien Springs, MI 49103, 1985.

————. *Bird Studies.* Publication of David Mohrhardt, 314 N. Bluff, Berrien Springs, MI 49103, 1986.

Pearson, T. Gilbert, ed. *Birds of America.* Garden City Publishing Co., 1936.

Peck, Robert McCracken. *A Celebration of Birds.* Walker and Co., 1982.

Peterson, Roger Tory. *A Field Guide to the Birds.* Houghton Mifflin Co., 1980.

Poole, Robert M., ed. *The Wonder of Birds.* National Geographic Society, 1983.

Porter, Eliot. *Birds of North America: A Personal Selection.* A&W Visual Library.

Schroeder, Roger. *How to Carve Wildfowl.* Stackpole Books, 1984.

Scott, Peter. *Key to the Wildfowl of the World.* Wildfowl Trust, 1957.

————. *Observations of Wildfowl.* Cornell University Press, 1980.

Shortt, Michael Terence. *Wild Birds of the Americas.* Pagurian Press, 1977.

Simon, Hilda. *The Splendor of Iridescence.* Dodd, Mead & Co., 1971.

Small, Anne. *Masters of Decorative Bird Carving.* Winchester Press, 1981.

Snow, David, Chisholm, A. H., and Soper, M. F. *Raymond Ching: The Bird Paintings.* William Collins & Co., 1978.

Spaulding, Edward S. *Quails.* MacMillan.

Stefferud, Alfred, ed. *Birds in Our Lives.* Arco Publishing Co., 1970.

Stepanek, O. *Birds of Heath and Marshland.* West Book House, 1962.

Terres, John K. *The Audubon Society Encyclopedia of North American Birds.* Alfred A. Knopf, 1980.

Tunnicliffe, Charles. *A Sketchbook of Birds.* Holt, Rinehart and Winston, 1979.

Van Wormer, Joe. *The World of the Swan.* J.B. Lippincott Co., 1972.

Wetmore, Alexander, ed. *Song and Garden Birds of North America.* National Geographic Society, 1964.

Zim, Herbert, and Sprunt, Alexander. *Game Birds.* Western, 1961.

Magazines of Interest to Wildfowl Carvers:

Breakthrough Magazine, P.O. Box 1320, Loganville, GA 30249.

Chip Chats, The National Woodcarvers' Association, 7424 Miami Ave., Cincinnati, OH 45243.

The Living Bird Quarterly, Laboratory of Ornithology at Cornell University, 159 Sapsucker Woods Rd., Ithaca, NY 14850.

Wildfowl Art, Journal of the Ward Foundation, 655 S. Salisbury Blvd., Salisbury, MD 21801.

Wildfowl Carving and Collecting, Box 1831, Harrisburg, PA 17105.

Other fine carving books from Stackpole Books

Waterfowl Carving With J.D. Sprankle
The fully illustrated reference to carving and painting 25 decorative ducks
by Roger Schroeder and James D. Sprankle

How to Carve Wildfowl
9 North American Masters Reveal the Carving and Painting Techniques that Win Them International Blue Ribbons
by Roger Schroeder

How to Carve Wildfowl Book 2
Best-in-Show Techniques of 8 Master Bird Carvers
by Roger Schroeder

Wildlife Woodcarvers
A Complete How to Do It Book for Carving, Burning, and Painting Wildfowl
by Carl Chapell and Clark Sullivan

Woodcarving Illustrated
Easy-to-carve projects pictured in step-by-step diagrams; Complete with detailed painting instructions
by Roger Schroeder and Paul McCarthy

Woodcarving Illustrated Book 2
8 Useful Projects You Can Carve Out of Wood
by Paul McCarthy/Roger Schroeder